YOUR
SALON TEAM

The salon owner's guide to finding, motivating and keeping great staff

LISA CONWAY

Published by Zing Office in 2018. First Published 2016.

© Lisa Conway 2015

All rights reserved. The moral right of the author has been asserted. No part of this book may be reproduced by any person or entity, including internet search engines or retailers, in any form or by any means, electronic or mechanical, including photocopying (except under the statutory exceptions provisions of the Australian Copyright Act 1968), recording, scanning or by any information storage retrieval system without the prior written permission of the publisher.

Title: Your Salon Team: The salon owner's guide to finding, motivating and keeping great staff / Lisa Conway.

ISBN: 9780646958354 (pbk.)

Subjects: Beauty shops--Australia--Management.
Hairdressing--Australia--Management.
Success in business--Australia.

Disclaimer
The material in this publication is of the nature of general comment only, and does not represent professional advice. It is not intended to provide specific guidance for particular circumstances and it should not be relied on as the basis for any decision to take action or not take action on any matter which it covers. Readers should obtain professional advice where appropriate, before making any such decision. The author and publisher disclaim all responsibility and liability to any person, arising directly or indirectly from any person taking or not taking action based on the informaton in this publication.

Photography: Jason Malouin www.portraitstore.com.au
Editor: Sheryl Allen www.sherylallencopy.com
Illustrations: Timothy Davis tim@brassantlers.com
Layout & book cover: Michelle Pirovich www.thesqueezebox.com.au

To Aaron, Jacob and Tess.
"Team Family"
– my best work yet.

Contents

Foreword   9

Preface   11

1. Why you need to hear this and why you need to start with you.   21
2. Google, gather and go – networking with your industry tribe.   41
3. Would you work for you? The Self Checklist.   55
4. The Team Hokey Pokey – is that what it's all about?   75
5. Safety in numbers – why a bigger team is a better team.   85
6. Hiring who you need, when you need (it's about mandarins and oranges).   93
7. Where to advertise and how to write a winning job ad.   109
8. Passion versus skill: going deep during the interview and those first few weeks.   123
9. When your salon's a family affair.   137
10. The miracle of motivation and upping an attitude score.   149
11. The problem: is it you or them? Are you being too flexible?   163
12. Targets: why, what, when and how?   179

Contents

13 What meerkats and Indian givers can teach you about sharing the load and motivating your team. 193

14 Creating a negative-free salon zone – we all just want to have fun. 205

15 Prepare to parent (because you will). 219

16 Your salon's culture – setting clear expectations and tackling tough topics. 227

17 Why they're leaving you and what should you do … pay more, talk more or let them go? 241

18 Get clear on who your clients belong to. 259

19 Is there a potential salon manager or partner in your midst? 273

20 Stop beating yourself up. You can learn to lead your tribe. 285

21 Tits up, in a good way? 297

*"Great teams are founded on two things:
truth and training – in that order."*

Lisa Conway

Foreword

"Give it a year." That's what Lisa said and that's what we've done. It's just on 12 months since I first met Lisa and welcomed her into our salon.

If you're a salon owner, I promise you'll find at least one huge take-away within these pages that will change the way you manage your business.

What's changed for us since Lisa arrived? Everything and nothing. We're still a large salon in Fitzroy, Melbourne without a streetfront. We're still true to our vision and passionate about what we do. The difference is: we're now confident and in control of our business and our team. We're happy with all 17 people on our team. We not only have goals, we know how to achieve them.

After three years in business, we knew we needed to improve but we didn't know how. We always tried to please our staff because we valued them and we feared the impact of them leaving. Our staff turnover was low but our team was doing their own thing rather than what we wanted them to do. As Lisa put it, "It's like you're all on different islands. We need to get you on the same island."

Lisa helped us resolve challenges quickly through clever strategies, education and reassurance. She gets us. She gets our industry. Her depth of experience shines through and her respectful yet down-to-earth manner makes her easy to be around.

How fast did it happen? We saw big results within three months. Lisa showed us how to prioritise our team challenges, who and what to work on first. She taught us the importance of knowing our numbers. Before Lisa, we had no idea how many people walked through our doors each week. Now we track everything and everyone on our team knows and understands their figures.

Overall, we've sharpened our team (reducing it by three) while increasing our turnover. We feel happy with every person working for us. There's a real sense of them coming along with us on the journey. We're all on the same island.

We've never been more confident about our business future, knowing we have the skills we need to keep growing, improving and dealing with new challenges as they arise. We no longer panic about a shift in staff; we know how to manage it. We're getting excited about the potential to expand into a second salon. Mostly we love that our clients now get consistently great service and have all their hair needs met, while we remain true to our values.

Your Salon Team goes even deeper than Lisa's first book *The Naked Salon*, drilling down into what makes a team really work. Like Lisa, this book is clever, generous and full of know-how. It's fun and down-to-earth – easy to have around. Read it, do it … and give it a year.

Bianca Villella

Preface

What I do know after 30 years in this industry is this: "It is as it is".

You either get it or you don't.

Some of my fondest memories in life have been my connection with my salon clients and my salon team. To this day, I'll be out somewhere and I'll see someone who used to be on my team or a past salon client and I always go over and smile because I know that the workplace I provided and the service I delivered was my best. I would never have to cross the road or duck my head down for fear of being recognised.

If you're honest with yourself and your team, you can't go wrong. I think coming from a small country town and growing up in a family of nine kids, I just learnt that you get caught out being dishonest. Honesty is one of my strengths I've always brought to my team.

One of my culture points has always been: *At this salon, we want you to feel proud of your work. When you have a win we'd love to know about it so we can share it with you. We also want to know when you "stuff something up" so we can guide you out of trouble and help you avoid it happening again.*

The trouble is we spend too much time trying to fit in, trying to be something or someone, wanting to be liked. It's not until we get older that we start to truly accept who we are.

I can remember when I was younger, perhaps in my 30s, reading articles about women in their 50s saying they've never been happier. Even though they were older now, and perhaps their bodies were showing it, their minds were more at ease. All of their experiences – good, bad or indifferent – make up the person they are today.

I've always been a confident person. People have always remarked that I knew what I wanted and that I was focused and driven, sometimes exhausting, to be around.

But I didn't realise how much I cared about what people thought of me until I opened up my first salon and started building a team.

I wasn't really aware that I was trying to please everyone with my actions. All I knew was life was better when my girls in the salon were getting along. Life was better when my clients left the salon happy. Life was better when my husband was in a good mood. Life was better when my kids weren't fighting over their toys. Life was better when my friends were happy with the movie choice and the food in the restaurant was to their liking.

I'm easy-going when it comes to what makes me happy. I'm attracted to people who are consistently in a good mood. I treasure funny people. When asked who I'd run off with, I'd nominate Billy Connolly because I find happiness and a sense of humour so attractive.

What I hadn't given much thought to was how difficult it is and how much energy it takes to keep everyone happy. It's a lot like a juggler trying to keep all the balls in the air.

I know for sure that you need to be really clear on the vision and direction of your salon and go about finding great people to support your vision.

You may not agree with everything you're about to read in this book. But I'm sure you'll agree with me when I say you need to paint a picture of what you want to get done. Creating that picture or blueprint is what you can do much better.

Each of us can be more engaging with our team, everyone can be a clearer leader and we can all motivate our team more than we do. Your challenge is to paint a bigger picture and get your team to join in when the painting starts. That's the surest sign of a great leader – that others are following along and joining in the painting, taking ownership of the change, the process and the outcome.

A wise man who lived in a time when most leaders were "he" once put it like this:

A leader is best when people barely know he exists, when his work is done, his aim fulfilled, they will say: we did it ourselves. (Lao Tzu)

Stop making excuses for your team and settling for average. When you do, it rolls down the hill and your clients get average, too. That's not what you set out to do when you opened your salon.

Be honest with yourself.

Not one of you is reading this book because you suddenly decided: *I know. I'll open up a hair salon or beauty salon because I think I can just be average.*

Like me, you've seen situations where people were average and you know you can do better than that.

So get on with it! Don't waste 10 years working it out. Find someone to help you.

The Cinderella syndrome.

I remember back to my Saturdays working on the salon floor. On those special days – weddings, big race meetings, events – clients would be coming in to have their hair done and it felt like everyone was going somewhere, except me. One lot were heading off to a wedding, another lot to a fashion show, another to some other fancy occasion. I'd be there doing their hair, being busy, making cups of coffee, finding a bandaid for someone, getting some nail polish remover for someone who hadn't had time to take her polish off. I was certainly the support person. Then they'd all leave and I'd be left standing there holding my tail comb.

I used to feel like Cinderella – like everyone was off to the ball except me. By the time I'd finished making my clients feel fabulous and sent them off to wherever they were going, I was exhausted and left with a pile of towels to take home and launder. So what changed? I learned that I had to make time for me so I didn't lurch straight from the busy-ness of the salon to more busy-ness at home. I needed to feel good about myself, too – even if I wasn't going to the ball! I resolved it by always having a simple time-out for me after a busy day. I might head around to a café to sit and read the paper for half an hour, or take my dog for a walk in the park. I needed to de-frag and unwind, to make time for me. The more time I made for me, the more I felt in control of my business and my personal life. I was less like Cinderella left behind to sweep up the cinders and more like a glammed-up girl heading off to the ball in my glass heels.

Making time for you when you're a busy salon owner takes courage and planning. And I mean REAL time. Not thirty minutes snatched here and there. I'm always talking about time, team and money. That's for good reason. I'm 100% certain that if you're ever going to have time for yourself, you need to be making more money. If you're not making the money you desire and deserve, then you need to start making it happen. And you must start with your team.

You may not even have a team. You may be reading this book thinking: *How do I start? When do I get a team together? How do I choose that first person?*

Most of you are frightened to get a team member for fear they won't work out. It's fear that's holding you back.

I hope this book shows you that you can overcome your fear and learn how to gather and lead your tribe. I want that for you, too.

You can have a successful salon that gives you the money and life choices you deserve.

You just need to have a strong vision, be prepared to communicate, to be honest with yourself and those around you. And, you need to ask for the help you need.

You already have a good salon and there's never been a better time to start taking your salon, your team and yourself from good to great!

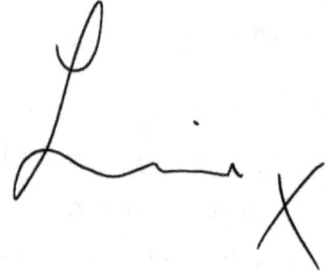

chapter 1

1

1

Why you need to hear this and why you need to start with you.

It's more than five years since I sold my last salon, yet I still jump out of bed on a Saturday morning excited that no one is going to call in sick. I think back to my early days as a salon owner when an early morning phone call meant a sinking feeling in the pit of my stomach. Chaos was about to swallow my Saturday.

Like me, you probably hadn't imagined that managing your salon team was going to be such a big gig. That, at times, it'd consume you 24/7.

Now I know the truth and it's part of the bigger picture you need to hear. Someone taking a sickie is all part of owning a business – and there are ways to manage the chaos, even on a busy Saturday.

1

Owning a business is a game for grown-ups and grown-ups make plans. They learn what they need to know and they take responsibility for making things happen.

Tell me: what's your plan? What's the difference between today and the same day one year from now? Do you even have one? Perhaps it's in your head, buried amongst your other thoughts. *Need to book the car for a service. Have to email my stock order. What time are tonight's parent-teacher interviews?*

My guess is you have a whole lot going on.

So, you need a clear plan. Every business owner needs a plan. You're going to need a plan for each and every person on your team. But the biggest plan is for you, because you hold your team together. In this book, I'm going to tell you how.

The salon team is one of our industry's biggest challenges. Perhaps you're struggling with your existing team, making do with what you have, believing this is as good as it gets. And that's my first challenge – your mindset. If you believe this is as good as it gets, you are 100% correct. If you think a better way is possible and that there are great people out there who you can invite to join your awesome team, then you are also correct.

Just stop doing what my father called "trying to make a silk purse out of a sow's ear." I was lucky enough to grow up on a farm where everything had an animal-related metaphor. Most of my common sense approach to life and the hair and beauty industry comes from that organic upbringing.

1

I'm a city-dweller now, but I've never been clearer about my role on this planet. As you read on you'll continue to find yours. You'll get crystal clear on where you need to focus your energy – on your team. For without a great team you will always struggle for time and money.

> **"Owning a business is a game for grown-ups"**

Grow yourself first and your team second.

Once, when I went home to the country to visit my parents, my mum and I decided to make an early start for a road trip to visit my sister in Mildura. Just before we left, Mum snuck back into her bedroom to get some cash from the pockets of Dad's trousers. I looked in to see if Dad was awake to say goodbye. He was lying on his back on white sheets wearing a white singlet. With his very pale white skin he looked like a ghost. His mouth was wide open and he was snoring so loud I swear the curtains were being sucked in and blown out by the incredible sound of each breath. I was staring at him with a shocked look on my face, when Mum turned to me and said, "It didn't happen overnight you know. He was quite the catch once, actually a very handsome man and a good dancer". Then she started to giggle. All I could think was, "He seems to be hiding it quite well now".

1

Mum was absolutely right (she always was). Time does slip away on us. None of us is getting any younger so there's never been a better time to do what you have to do to make the money you deserve. One year, 10 years or 20 years from now, you could be in a financial position you're proud of. You just have to start. Now.

The same goes for each of your salon team members. By giving them the right attention now, you can help them grow toward meeting their potential. At the same time, you'll be growing yourself and your business.

Most people don't have a mentor or a coach meaning most people aren't aware of just how awesome they actually are or could be. They're just bopping along on their merry (or not so merry) way. The trouble with bopping along is that time gets away from you. Things like a milestone birthday or a school reunion have you stopping in your tracks thinking: *What the hell? How did I get here?*

I don't know how to stop time. Everyone, eventually, will end up snoring like my dad did that day. What I do know is that every year you don't grow your business to its full potential, every time you procrastinate about what it is you should be doing to grow it, you are wasting precious time. Don't wait around for your energy to kick-in – there is nothing as energising as action.

1

Plan for tomorrow. Action it today.

In your salon, growing good people means that you have to get involved, you have to find out what they want. The simplest way is to ask them: *In one year from today, what do you want to have learnt? What do you want to have completed or ticked off?*

Your job as leader is to work back from their answers and set a plan into action. It might be that they'd like to work more hours than they're working now. Perhaps they'd like to be working less while getting the same pay. What are the changes and what are the actions they need to get done in order to get the outcomes they want? I suggest once you have your list, start with the easiest ones first, so you can all feel the buzz of early wins.

Here's an example of action planning for a team member who wants to be able to confidently spray tan and turn the tan room around for the next client, all in 15 minutes. Your action from today could be: *We're now looking for 10 models who we can spray tan at half price to test the time and quality. Let's find five models for this week and five for next and then reassess the skills.*

Don't overcomplicate it. Just do it. One step at a time.

Get hooked on the doing.

I know changes come from an emotion, any emotion – the positive ones like excitement, nervous energy, anticipation and also the not-so-good ones like tears, frustration and anger.

The deeper the emotion, the stronger the changes.

When I start mentoring a new salon, I do a 90-minute discovery session to look at their figures and see if we're a good match to work together. At the end of the session, I always ask if the salon owner: *Do you have any questions? Now that you have a clearer picture of your business, what are you feeling?*

Unless they're feeling a strong sense of emotion, then I'm worried. For my money, the "perfect storm" of emotions is excitement, relief and fear, but I'll take any show of feeling at this stage. If we're going to work together, you need to be feeling something. The same goes for your salon teams – you need them to invest in the business emotionally. If they feel nothing toward the business, chances are they don't care. My favourites are the ones who feel enough to come to you with ideas and plans, no matter how whacky. They're invested and that's always a good thing.

In order to change, you need to be so frustrated or mentally exhausted that you want the change bad. The next step is translating those emotions into positive ones so you can develop a new level of energy and excitement around what you're going to be doing next.

People are attracted to energy, good or bad. Others pick up so much from your body language. Be aware that you're mentoring your team every single time they see you. For some of you, this is way too much pressure you hadn't factored in when you decided to be the salon owner.

1

For others, it's just what you do. You look your best every day. You add value to everyone who crosses your path. You can't wait to get on with your day and tick those tasks off your to-do list. Every day has huge value to you and you act accordingly. Or maybe this doesn't sound like you, but it's exactly where you want to be as a leader? Let me tell you, it's 100% worth it. If, as the leader of your business, you don't know what the next move is, you haven't got a hope in hell of getting your team to follow you on the journey of change.

Everyone needs a plan. Everyone who works in your business needs to be following a plan – it might as well be yours. Telling people what to do doesn't work. Engaging people in a discussion and coming up with a plan together does.

Growing good people from where they are now requires you to have a good plan. It needs to be specific and clear-cut. So, for example, you can be saying to a team member, "This time next year, this business needs a full-time senior operator and I believe you're right for the job. We need to make a plan around how we make that happen for you. You are my next senior and I'm confident you're going to be a great one. Let's get a plan together and action that plan. What are the things you need to learn or be able to master so that you can step-up into that role this time next year?"

You're allowed to expect (and ask for) more.

Are you fooling yourself that nobody is going to treat your business as well as you do? That's absolute rubbish. The problem is that most of you are settling for mediocrity. You accept average performances from people who are capable of way more. You're scared to do what it takes to lead them for fear it doesn't work. Because you don't know what to do then. *Do I push them? What if they hate me? What if it's already the best they can do?*

> *None of us is getting any younger so there's never been a better time to do what you have to do.*

Trust me on this: everyone is capable of much, much more, including you. That's where the real problem starts – with you. You think you need to push them, when what you really need to do is inspire them to be more.

Yet, you've never been taught how. You've not had a single lesson in how to motivate and inspire people to greatness. So, stop being so hard on yourself. Lighten up and read on, because that's about to change.

1

Enjoy the journey of change this book will set you on. Soak up the OMG! and aha! moments. At times, you'll wonder if I've been in your head. In a way, I have …

I know your mindset is what holds you back because I had the same mindset before Bruce, my first mentor, challenged me. I was so emotionally involved and knew that much about my team's personal lives that I made excuses for them before they did. I put everyone else ahead of what I really wanted to achieve in my business. Sound familiar?

Now I know the single best thing you can do for your team is create a safe workplace, free of bullies' discrimination and full of fabulous clients who make your life a joy. You can't do that if you're weighed down with every personal problem brought to work. Your job is to wow your team as a boss. Their job is to wow the clients as a professional on your salon team. More about that later.

Stop with the "that's just her".

While reading this book, you'll naturally think about your current team. One-by-one, I want you look at the qualities each has and do a review. Everyone on your team needs a review. Everyone. Even you. No one is exempt.

Tempted to overlook a particular team member because "that's just her"? Then, she's the one you probably need to focus on hardest. Let me scratch a tad deeper and tell you a story to explain your "that's just her" thinking and how it's costing you money.

1

Lucy was working in Joel's salon. They'd been colleagues in another life and their working relationship spanned almost 20 years. Lucy virtually did her own roster and came and went as she pleased. Joel said she brought in good money. When I looked closer at Lucy's figures, I found her average dollar sale was quite low, considering she and Joel were on the same price point. I also noticed that less than 25% of her clients rebooked their next appointments. They were loyal clients, but they were very hit and miss.

Compared to others on the team, Lucy had no trouble arriving on time or behaving professionally. But I knew if we were to change the salon culture, Lucy had to be included – the *one in, all in* rule. Joel was nervous because, in his words: "she hates change". It fascinates me that we so easily accept behaviours from people.

After a long conversation with Lucy, it was clear she believed (or actually knew) that her clients wouldn't pay extra for retail or basin services/treatments and that they don't like to commit to booking their next appointment. She said they had kids so just called to arrange a time when it suited.

Yes, you heard me – "they had kids" was the excuse. I bet these mums routinely re-book their kids' other activities. Imagine them saying to the tennis instructor or the ballet teacher: "I'll call you when I need you." It comes down to the value you place on people and things. It's just how it is.

Your Salon Team 31

1

In my experience, when you show people how to behave, most will. If you don't believe that you, as a stylist or therapist, add incredible value to your clients, then they won't either.

Lucy was also doing some serious discounting for the clients she felt couldn't afford the full price. It took me a few goes to help her understand that each time she discounted, the business owner took a pay cut. Over her two days every week, it added up to more than $130 a week. $130 X 52 = $6,760! Over a year, it meant Joel could take an annual holiday, pay for training sessions for every one on the team or a hundred other things. And that's just one part-time employee.

I knew that, with my teachings, Lucy could stop the exhausting "head game" of deciding on their behalf what her clients could or couldn't afford to pay. She'd be freed up to just get on with her job and be the creative professional she truly is.

> *The problem is that most of you are settling for mediocrity.*

When I returned in a month's time, she was grinning ear-to-ear. She explained that some of her clients happily had basin services and were unconcerned that the discount had stopped.

Most of them growled at her for discounting in the first place. They had no idea they were even getting a discount.

Over three months we raised her average dollar sale by $35 and she weeded out some seriously D-grade clients. It wasn't that hard. Lucy was a seasoned and confident stylist who hadn't been challenged for years and I loved hearing her say: "Anyway, bugger them. You are 100% correct, I'm worth every cent. I just needed the lesson from you."

What's the lesson from this story? It's a biggie and you'll learn more about it as you read through this book. In a nutshell, taking things personally gets you nowhere. Learn to take out the emotion before you make decisions about your salon. You'll be left with the facts and it's so much easier to decide based on facts.

Don't ever forget who owns your business, whose head is on the chopping block. It's not Lucy's business; it's yours. People like Lucy don't set out to rip you off, but they do. So, stand up and protect it like it's your livelihood, because it is! The success you have here could mean the difference between sending your children to a public or a private school, or spending your annual holiday in a tent or a swish five-star hotel. And … in case you're wondering … I don't do tents, darling.

1

Give it a year.

It's going to take a shift. For some, it's going to take a huge shift. Some of you will have to throw a cat amongst the pigeons. There will be tears. There are always tears. Here's the truth. Some of the people who work with you now like or even *love* that you settle for mediocrity. They will fight for the right for everything to remain exactly the way it is.

In this book, I'm going to teach you that you need to master a big skill to lead a great salon team – you need to learn how to be an open, honest and transparent communicator. That one thing has the power to take you from where you are today to a much better place this time next year. Yes, it takes about 12 months to completely change the culture in any hair or beauty salon. You have clients to consider and you need to give everyone an opportunity to grow with you before you decide who's the right fit to move forward with you. Those sitting on the fence need to make a decision. They need to get in the pigs' pen with you (see my country roots). They need to roll up their sleeves for the team or "calm their farm" and find somewhere else to be average.

You're reading this book because you want to know how to develop an awesome salon team that will work whether or not you're there reminding and watching them. Why haven't you done it before? Because you don't know how to move on.

The good news is I'm going to leave no stone unturned. After reading this book you'll feel empowered and know exactly where and what to do to improve your salon team. The bad news is the person who has to change the most is you. You're going to put a mirror up to yourself, have a long hard look and decide whether or not this gig is really for you.

Let's get started.

I'm a GSD kind of girl – *Get Stuff Done* or *Get Shit Done*, whatever you like. Let's do this. I want you to grab a notebook and write down all the qualities that you know a great team member has. As you read this book, you'll look back at this list and sharpen it like the edge of a knife. The blunt knife you're using now might cut, but you have to use force. A super sharp knife will slice through your team challenges and you'll find life isn't the hard push it used to be.

I ask you to begin to change your thinking and don't ever settle for less. You might not want to hear this, but … you get the staff you deserve. Ouch! Your challenge is to deserve and expect more. Every day. Every team member. Every decision.

Now, grab a highlighter and a pen and as you read, write all over this book. Tear out a page or three to pin on your salon staff room door. There are prizes for the most loved, read and re-read copy. The more dog-eared the better. I've seen a couple of rippers of my first book *The Naked Salon*, even one that got dunked in a hot tub. Post your over-loved, over-read book on my Facebook page and I'll send you another for free!

1

The Nitty Gritty.

You haven't been taught what you need to know. Yet.

It takes time.

It starts with you. It's your business.

You need a plan.

Now is the right time to grow.

Don't wait for your energy to kick in – you can kick it in.

Ask the right questions – dig deeper.

Take the emotion out.

Expect more. Deserve it.

Plan for tomorrow and action it today.

Keep it simple. Just do it.

chapter 2

2

2

Google, gather and go.

I once knew a salon owner who was having trouble getting her team of three to understand the difference between what a client came to the salon for and what that client might really need (or want). They were baulking at recommending new products or services. And they definitely weren't offering solutions that were in line with being an expert and creating a special salon experience. Jay, one of the ZING coaches, suggested the team head along to an upcoming industry event, emphasising that they could look around as a team and maybe come back with something new to offer clients.

They took the opportunity to have some fun and stayed overnight in town, attending the industry show over two days. They came home with Ruffy mitts paraffin hand wax treatments and an array of other ideas for their clients to experience. They had a ball and because they went as a team, they all engaged in the decision-making and were on board and excited about the new products from day one, rather than being detached from the process when the salon owner previously went along solo to the event. The team energy soared and so did the sales.

That's just one way networking can benefit your salon and your team. There are dozens of reasons why you should be out getting up close and personal with your industry tribe.

Let's get one thing straight: you chose this industry. Right? Nobody twisted your arm and said you have to work in the hair and beauty industry. There was no voice of The Godfather imploring: "you have to do this; it's for the family".

Chances are, you came up with the idea all by yourself. That you had a calling or you just knew it was right for you. What you might not have known then is that it's an industry where you have to be engaged one hundred per cent of the time. If you're not, your credibility and following drops. Pronto.

Step up and step onto the salon stage.

Your salon floor or your beauty rooms are like the stage. It's show business and there's no business like it. You need to develop a "show must go on" mentality.

When you step onto the stage, the crowd expects a performance. Yes, you read that right – a performance from you. And, if you don't deliver a kick-butt performance, the review will be your downfall. Not in the same way as a normal theatre review, but in a silent review (the worst kind). Your public vote with their feet. In the world of theatre, they will applaud you with their hands and perhaps a call for an encore. With us, they vote with their feet. They might tolerate one lacklustre performance, but they won't bear multiple disappointments.

Like acting, your profession is a craft that takes skill and experience. To perform – and I mean *really* perform – you need to bring your best game, to know your stuff, to be in control of your salon and your team. So, how do you get your head in the right space to give your best performance every time? You engage wholeheartedly with your industry tribe. Yes, I mean networking.

> *You need to develop a "show must go on" mentality.*

Pump up your tyres. Top up your tank.

I come across salon owners who haven't been out to an industry event in more than 10 years. Maybe you're one of them. I ask you: how does that even work? How can you possibly perform at your best, be highly engaged, when you don't ever have your passion pumped up? To me, it's absolute madness.

You can't perform on song when you're running on your rims. When did you last check your tyre pressure? If you've ridden a bike, you know the pedalling's so much easier when your tyres are fully pumped. We're exactly the same. If you get out to industry events, you'll be the pumped-up, ready-to-roll version of yourself. You'll be ready for the matinee, the evening performance and all the encores. Get out amongst it. Stop making excuses.

In my book (and this is *my* book) you should be getting to one industry event a month. Yes, at least twelve of those buzzy, bubbly, tyre-pumping gatherings each year.

Networking is not a dirty word.

Write this on your fridge: *Google, gather and go.* Write it big and bold. Own it. Because that's exactly what you need to do. Get on the internet. Google "seminars, industry events for hair and beauty" or "what, who, when". Get your team excited and go. It's that simple. Once you've made industry gathering a business goal, you'll find a way to make it happen. Stop making excuses, procrastinating and second-guessing. Just go.

Not every event you attend will float your boat. Who cares? I've been to many restaurants and had some pretty ordinary meals. But I keep going back. I don't give up (nor do I ever plan to give up) eating out. I hedge my bets by being fussy about where I go. And you should, too. Apply the same principle to your off-site industry motivation or training nights as you do to choosing a restaurant.

You'll reap the rewards from attending a diverse range of events. You'll not only pump your tyres up, but you'll shift your thinking one hundred and eighty degrees. You'll be exposed to new ideas, new people, new trends, new techniques and you'll look at your own salon and team through new eyes.

The about-face in action.

You've arrived. The room is full of your industry tribe. These are your people. OK, some of them are out there. That's what makes the world twirl. This is a creative industry and the people-watching is always entertaining.

But don't forget why you're here. Focus on a specific outcome for the event. For example, I always strive to come away having made one connection and had one decent conversation with a like-minded person.

Networking is daunting, whatever way you look at it. So take a deep breath and put a plan into action. Take the first half hour to look around the room, see who you know, see who you don't and decide on that one person you're going to introduce yourself to. It's no different to being in your salon. You have only minutes to build a rapport. It's something you do well, every day, day in, day out. So, go with the flow and do the same.

You'll be surprised how easy hair and beauty folk are to talk to. It's almost like you're one of them. Hang on … you are! This is your tribe and you belong with these people. This is your professional campfire. If a stranger came up to you and said, "My name's Lisa. I own a salon in Parkville and I just thought to come over and say Hi," you'd respond in a friendly, welcoming manner, wouldn't you? So, why wouldn't you expect the same from your peers?

Another incentive: these industry events usually include alcohol and food. Not boring old food like chocolate mousse and sticky date pudding. It's not 1916! You can expect fancy, gourmet fare. I personally wouldn't think of running an event without bevies (in fact, they've become both a drawcard and a hallmark of ZING gatherings). Most event organisers I know concur. You work hard and deserve to relax with a drink in your hand and we all know how a bevie helps the conversation flow. The bonus is, you get to kick-back and enjoy yourself a little while you're learning and becoming better at what you do.

Don't give me that.

The gig's up guys. You have to crawl out from under the "I just don't have the time" rock and stop with the excuses. *They are never when it suits me. I didn't know it was on. Nobody to mind the kids. My dog hates being left all day and then all night.*

Blah, blah, blah. I've heard them all – and they *all* suck. Just pull your finger out and … Google, gather and go.

Ask your product company rep about any upcoming events. He or she will fall over with the shock and be genuinely delighted that you've changed your tune. He or she will go back to the office and take you out of the tired-grumpy-past-giving-a-hoot basket and pop you in the gives-a-shit-and-is-prepared-to-step-it-up-a-notch basket. Nice upgrade!

2

2

He or she will be excited for all sorts of reasons. I know first-hand how hard it is to fill a room. It's bloody formidable – you people are brim-full with empty excuses.

I get that. You talk all day and when you knock off you want to go home and switch off. But I also get that you always have a little more in that energy tank. You just have to make a conscious decision to reach deeper for it.

> **"You always have a little more in that energy tank. You just have to make a conscious decision to reach deeper for it."**

In cave man times they hunted and gathered all day, then sat and stared at the fire all night. We've just replaced the fire with the TV or some other screen device, or Facebook or iPads or the like. If you're a parent, you go home to the kids' readers, the laundry, tennis lessons and an endless list of daily chores. Don't I know it! I did that, too, and somehow managed.

But you're on a different path. You're reading this book because you want to make a difference to your salon's culture. You're interested in one or all three of these things: attracting, motivating or keeping great people. Attending industry events is a key element in making one or all of those things happen. You must get involved, engaged and in touch with your industry. It's your mission. Choose to accept it. Now … Google, gather and go!

The Nitty Gritty.

You chose this industry. Remember why.

To perform at your best, you must engage with your industry tribe.

You can't do your best when you're running on your rims.

Aim for one industry event a month (every month).

Stop making excuses (we've heard them all).

Go with a plan.

Relax and enjoy yourself.

Ask your product company rep about events.

Google, gather and go!

chapter 3

3

Would you work for you? The Self Checklist.

The other day I pulled up behind a salon I was going to mentor and saw one of the girls out the back having a break. "I'm really glad to see you here, Simone," I said. "Because when you first started here you were a bit wobbly." She smiled. "I know. I'm so glad I listened to you and stayed. I didn't realise then that I was working for a great boss but I know it now. At the start, I thought there were too many rules for me to ever enjoy working here. Now I get that the rules make it fair for everyone. We all know what's expected of us. We all know what to do. Because he's such a great boss, he has a great team and for me that means having another place where I feel like I belong. This is my work family."

It's true. Sometimes people don't get why we need the rules until you show them: to make it fair, to protect everyone, so there's no bullying and bitching. People want to be proud of where they work, to be confident about their role and to know they're valued. They want to work in a business that's going somewhere, that's profitable and has an owner who can manage the books. People who work in hair or beauty salons are no different. Who wants their pay to be at the mercy of the salon's cashflow or to be waiting months for their superannuation to be transferred?

To attract the best people to your team, you need to build yourself a reputation as an awesome boss. Then finding the right people won't be such a challenge. You'll be an employer of choice and the best people will come looking for you, in the same way people climb over each other to get a job with Apple or Google.

> **To attract the *best people* to your team, you need to build yourself a reputation *as an awesome boss.***

What makes a great boss in our industry? I've put together a list of the qualities that elevate you from average salon owner to amazing boss and team leader. How many can you honestly put a tick beside?

You have a vision and a plan

You have a big picture plan – beyond the day-to-day problems of running a salon. Many salon owners could get a job at the local fire brigade as they spend so much of their day "putting out fires", wasting so much time details, they never get to the big stuff. I think some of them actually sleep with the fire hose in their bed or a fire truck on stand-by, just to be ready for any little flare-up. I'm imagining an over-stressed salon owner asleep with one eye open and the fire hose under his arm. Bless.

If you have a vision, you can tell me what you're working on at any given time and why. You work toward an outcome, you have an eye for talent and can see potential in a person. You don't sweat the small stuff. You consistently move toward the end goal and get excited about how you will feel when you reach it. You know what you want and you're going to make it happen.

You care about your looks

You present yourself immaculately. Every day. You understand that you're part of an industry where appearance matters. Others admire your sense of style and you always look awesome. That means from head to toe, no chipped polish and no same-again-Sam makeup that's been repeated every morning for the last 10 years. You have it going on – a style that's a complete look, something I call photo-ready. At any point, the media (any media from anywhere) could swing open your salon door and say, "We have a huge celebrity here with us and we would like to take a few shots of him with a local trader. We thought you might be interested." Are you ready to pose with Jamie Fox, George Clooney or [insert your favourite celebrity crush]? Are you going to panic? No, you're going to say, "Love to. Just two seconds for my lip gloss and I'm good to go."

Your moods don't swing

You don't come to the salon packing multiple personalities. You're the same person every day of the year – you have time for everyone and always teaching someone something. It could be an eighty-something client how to login on Facebook or an apprentice how to hide a bobby pin in a hair-up. You welcome questions and answer clearly and precisely. No matter what day or what time of day it is, you greet your team with the same personality. You're what my dad would call a "good scout". If you can't do someone a good turn, you wouldn't do one at all.

You're on top of business admin

You have the business side of your salon covered. You understand the backend and know what is expected financially from your business. You reach all the basic requirements: super paid on time, payslips printed and all other expenses under control, creating an environment where creativity is the focus of every day. The product companies love you because you pay your accounts on time and are always interested in what's new and exciting. You insist that everyone gets their breaks so they're fresh to deliver a great customer experience.

You're a good listener

You listen to everyone's concerns and can prioritise them as urgent, important and "would be nice". You work down the list, while making time in your life for things that are neither pressing nor essential, but would make others feel good. Listening to your team's needs is important to you and you value communication. You insist on regular one-on-one meetings as well as the whole group together, so everyone gets to have a say. Everyone's point is valid. You stay calmly pleasant and in control, mediating common ground between what your team have to say and what your clients feel.

You get the work life balance thing

When your team ask for leave, you're genuinely excited for them to have their well-earned break. You understand that, in order for you to be an awesome leader, you also need to have time off to recharge your own batteries. You trust the team to continue when you're not there. You don't expect them to do anything you wouldn't do yourself. You're not a martyr – you trust people to help you and in return you help them. You know this makes you approachable and balanced.

You respect your time on the floor

You value what every one of your team does and would never ask any of them to do your friends or family at a discounted rate, or worse, for free without considering it into their target. You know the guidelines around such things are fairer to everyone and respect that your team are keen to reach their targets. You have in place a fair, easy-to-understand system for everything. When there's promotional work that's free or discounted, you factor it in to team targets. You adjust figures so no one loses or is disadvantaged. You constantly teach your smart work practices so you can delegate and not wear yourself out.

You value education

You're always training yourself, especially in personal development. You treasure a high standard of education, are a born leader and lead by example. You never pull out the "I'm too busy" card. You believe that in-house and off-site education are paramount and that there's a place for both. Finding out what's on where and narrowing the choices down for your team is all part of the job for you.

You're a networking worker bee

Your networking skills are incredible. Everywhere you go, you hand out the salon's card and bring more clients for your team to look after. You're always eager to share the salon's brand and are super proud of your business. You genuinely believe in the value of the services you offer. You have an infectious personality and you could sell ice to the Eskimos because you honestly believe they should experience another kind of ice – your ice. You sell your salon to anyone you meet and shamelessly promote your team's talent. You're totally proud of the business you run.

> **You sell your salon to anyone you meet and *shamelessly promote your team's talent.*"**

You're honest

You support each of your team and you support the business. From time to time, you stuff up (we're all human) but you never cover it up or lie about it. Instead, you're transparent and honest about what's really going on. If only the whole world were like that.

If you can honestly put a big tick beside every one of those qualities on my list, you get the prize for being an awesome boss and a reputation that will draw awesome people to work for you. This is the MAGIC that will draw people to you.

P.S. Maybe ask for someone else's opinion on this before settling back and waiting for the magic to happen?

Another word on honesty.

Although it was last on my list, honesty deserves a place at the very top. There's always a time and a place to say what's on your mind. But I know one of my best qualities when managing a team of people – including my own children (or "team family") – would be that I was honest. You never had to guess what I was thinking. Chances are, I just told you. Team members repeatedly told me that my honest style was refreshing. And I continue to hear that same praise from the salon owners I coach. Sometimes we're faced with bad days, tough issues or unpredictable people. We need to see the humour in the situation and learn from it rather than have it drag us down.

Sort it. Learn the lesson. Move on.

I'm not going to tell you it's easy to run a hair or beauty salon. It's not. But remember, you chose your path. At one point, you thought running a salon was a great idea. Remember back to why. You did it because you know you can do this. Yes, it's often more difficult than you imagined. But if it were easy, every Tom, Dick and Harriet would be doing it.

Your focus needs to be squarely on your team. Without the right team, you're wasting time even bringing new clients through the salon door. They'll only slip out the back, never to be seen again. It's an expensive exercise and disastrous for your "word of mouth" referrals. Your service reputation is everything.

With the right team – and they're out there, believe me – you'll love running a salon. It's awesome fun! The diversity of clients you see and getting to make them feel and look beautiful is a wonderful thing to do for a living. I can't imagine working anywhere else. I loved my 25 years on the floor.

I used to laugh to my non-hairdressing friends and say it's like seeing all your favourite people, one by one. They make an appointment, they always come to you and the more beautiful you make them feel, the more money they give you. You call that a job? Really?

Creating the right team environment.

The one thing that will set you apart from your competitors is a genuine, happy working environment. You know the saying about marriage: "happy wife, happy life". Well, salon ownership is a case of "happy team, happy bank balance". I know, it doesn't rhyme, but it's true.

It's impossible to learn when you're unhappy. Your head is so preoccupied with the challenge you're working on, that you can't take on anything else. Ask anyone who works in education – that's why they work so hard on giving students proper meals and an environment where they're happy and feel safe. So they can actually focus enough to learn something. Children from troubled families and a poor quality of home life find it extremely hard to learn because the stress and sadness overwhelms and takes priority.

You can develop an awesome team environment. Focus on two things: the truth and the training. These will take you from where your business is today to where you know it can be.

Most people aren't truthful about the effort they put in personally. They lack motivation and direction. Most gloss over the truth. It's not until you look yourself in the mirror and say, "I can do better. I am going to be the best boss I can possibly be" that things will start to change.

> *Focus on two things: the truth and the training.*

You can start a change process by looking physically different. By that, I mean taking extra time to present yourself well. Maybe for you it means looking at your diet or your wardrobe, not to mention your hair and makeup. The minute you decide you can do better by putting in an extra effort, things will change for you.

You are what you eat and *you feel how you look*. Look great and you feel great. Look sick and you feel sick. Look shit and you feel like shit. People treat you how you look. Think about that for ten minutes. When have you recently been treated well or poorly and how were you presented at the time? Interesting, isn't it?

Once, I was sitting in a café in Ballarat and a young chap came up to me and asked if I'd mind staying a little longer and being in a photo for his website. He was happy for me not to pay for my coffee and whatever else I wanted. He had a sign on the door saying: *Closed for 30 minutes for a photo shoot.* He screened the people who tried to enter and the stylish ones got to come in. Do you think he would have asked me to be a part of this had I not been my stylish self? I watched on as he turned away some very plain Janes. Just saying. And, yes, I so had the cake!

The way you look determines the way you're treated. Right or wrong, it's the truth. I'm often asked why I wear such high heels. The reason is simple: they make me feel different to when I'm wearing flats, plus God made me short so I'm fixing his whoops. I'm in my early 50s and most of my girlfriends have given up on heels. They have their reasons and I'm sure they're valid. But for me, I feel like me in heels.

I chose this industry 30 years ago because of the way someone made me feel when I had a haircut at the age of 19. I get that same buzz today from wearing heels – it feels right. To me, it's the little things that we won't compromise on that make us unique.

Hair, heels and everything in between make you, you. Don't ever let anyone turn you into anything else. Be honest to your core and fight for the right to be you. When you're truly honest with yourself about the things you love and the things you don't, you will find like-minded people who support you. Work harder on yourself and you will find things falling into place and great people drawn to you. That's a great place to be in this business.

Why your team should be more talented than you.

Have you heard of the auntie syndrome? I have 22 nieces and nephews, and when I first became an auntie, I didn't give the auntie syndrome much thought. It wasn't until I was at one of my niece's weddings and they were all there looking glamorous and I thought: *When did this happen? When did I become the auntie who is shorter than my nieces and needs her glasses to read a text message on her iPhone!* And to have these girls, now in their twenties, giving me tips on where to look for the latest and coolest places to shop for clothes. It seems like yesterday I was showing them how to wear a scarf or coordinate shoes with an outfit. Now the tables have turned – they know way more about fashion than I do. In simple terms, they grew past me. And that's exactly as it should be.

And that's exactly as it should be in your salon, with your up and coming team members growing past you in terms of talent and know-how. I'd just prefer you planned it rather than have it catch you unawares as my nieces did with me.

We both know you want to work a little less on the floor and spend some more time either growing your business or just getting to all the things you're expected to do – that's why you're reading this book, right? If you want to have things done and dusted within business hours you need a plan of action.

Many of you find it difficult to cut back on your floor hours because you feel you have no one to look after your clients as well as you do. It feels like a giant risk to hand them over to anyone else and the whole idea causes you stress. Often, you don't find out things haven't worked for you until months later when the truth shows up and you think to yourself: *I haven't seen such-and-such for a while.*

There are probably two parts to this issue. First, the technical part – are your team members capable of delivering an exceptional skill set? Second, the care factor – do they have attention to detail down pat? The solution to both parts lies with you: employ people with passion and train everyone on your team to be better than you in every area possible.

When it comes to other things in your life, you're always looking for someone with more knowledge than you. Would you seek out a dance instructor who doesn't dance as well as you? Would you engage a bookkeeper who knows less about bookkeeping than you? (Please tell me your bookkeeper keeps better books than you?) And, you'd be crazy to take on a driving instructor who wasn't a better driver than you.

So, why the hell do you settle for less at work? I know, you're probably just hoping to find someone who can do a half-decent job and look after your clients half as good as you and rebook them like you do. I won't deny it's a difficult time to employ in our industry. But there are good people out there and some of you are settling for way less talent than you should be. Instead, take a "one-better" approach with everyone on your team – even when it comes to the way somebody dresses, find someone who has more flair or more style than you do. Another example is computer skills and the ability to manage social media – find people who have more skills than you.

Always aim high, especially when it comes to team members. It's not that you aim too high and miss, it's that most of you aim too low and hit it. I'll say it again: you won't want to hear this, but – you get the staff you deserve. I went from not being able to find anyone decent, to having people dropping off a CV when I didn't have the chairs for another team member. All because I worked harder on developing a fantastic environment to work in … and word spread.

Every time someone is more talented than you, your clients will happily have their services with them. That's the secret to team. Develop yourself a great team who are willing to share the load. This will free you up to concentrate on other aspects of your business.

Your other option is to train people up to have more skills than you. Someone might come to you who is equal to you when it comes to your core talent – in this case, it might be cutting. Instead of you being the one who goes off and does the latest cutting course, I suggest that ideally you both should go or, if that's not possible, send them along. When you see the confidence they gain from training and the energy they bring back into the salon, you'll understand the advantage. It's truly priceless and can go a long way to helping you attract and keep clientele.

> **You won't want to hear this, but – *you get the staff you deserve.***

When they return, they need to share what they learn with the whole team. Too many salon owners are overstretched and they suffer. If you add up the hours they put in they actually have two jobs. The trouble is: they being paid for only one. It's all a bit shit, to be honest!

The solution is to share the load, both on the salon floor and also in the day-to-day running of the business. I've never met a team member who didn't step-up and deliver what we asked once they understood the value we placed on being in a team. Often people don't step-up because they feel there is someone in their way, that they're in someone else's shadow. Usually, it's the salon owner's shadow.

The Nitty Gritty.

Great bosses attract awesome people to work for them.

Do you have what it takes to be a great boss?

Be honest. Be honest. Be honest.

Create the right team environment with truth and training.

People treat you how you look.

Plan to grow your team's skills beyond your own.

Look for talent when you're hiring.

Train up for talent from within.

Share the load.

chapter 4

4

The Team Hokey Pokey – is that what it's all about?

Imagine you have a child and, when he turns five, he goes to school. He does his first year. Then he does the next year of primary school. The following year, he does another, so he's now completing Grade 3. Then he stops – right there in Grade 3. He stops growing and learning so his teacher suggests he'd be better off repeating Grade 3. And that's what you let him do – repeat Grade 3. At the end of the year, the teacher recommends that he repeats Grade 3. Again. Now, aren't you burning to know what's halting his progress? Why can't he advance into Grade 4?

Why am I telling you this? Because, time and again, I see salon owners like you making progress in leaps and bounds in your first, second and third years in business. Then, for some reason, you lose momentum and end up stuck, repeating the same year over and over again.

Why? And why always the third year in business? There are many reasons. But mostly you're tired. Having two jobs – running a business *and* working in the business – turns out to be exhausting and few can manage it for more than a couple of years before visible cracks appear. Three years seems to be the point at which momentum slows down and many of you find yourselves stuck in a cycle of repeating the year before.

The other reason is you start to do what I call the *Team Hokey Pokey*. There's nothing graceful about this dance. Whatever team level you reach in the first few years, that's where you stay. You dance around, Hokey Pokey style, putting one team member in and then putting one team member out. You gain one, you lose one. You might be stuck at a team of five or a team of three, but wherever you got to during those first three years of business is pretty much where you'll hover. Surely, that *isn't* what it's all about?

To be successful, you need to keep on moving, keep on improving, keep on growing. I don't think you're ever done – progressing is just what you sign up for when you get into business.

Some of you might have got past your third-year team size at some stage. I applaud you, but I also know there's a good chance you've gone back to it, or are heading that way. I got to five and was stuck on five for a good few years until I engaged my first business coach. He helped me grow to a team of nine. But I will never forget how challenging it was to move on from the number five.

Whatever your situation, you need to accept that if you own a business, it either grows or dies a little bit each year. It will do one of those two things. Your challenge is to always keep it in a growing cycle. Stop telling yourself (and me) that you don't have enough space or enough clients to grow.

> *To be successful, you need to keep on moving, keep on improving, keep on growing*

If your excuse is that you have nowhere to fit new team members and you're only trading two nights a week and you're closed on a Monday, then you're not really trying. If you had great team members who were keen to work in your business, you could spread them out across a broader timeframe. Take another look at your appointment book and your salon resources. I bet you could probably fit in at least one more senior team member if you staggered the work over more days and evenings.

You could also think about growing into a new location. Either a second location to run in tandem with your current one, or relocating lock-stock-and-barrel to bigger premises with more basins, chairs or beauty rooms.

The number of clients you service every week will determine the number of team members you need. Refer to Chapter 6 for more detail on crunching those figures. To stay in a cycle of growth, you must be always – always! – actively and proactively marketing for new clients, as well as looking for your next team member. You need to work out what type of help you need most – a part-time receptionist, a full-time junior or someone to help you with the housework and the kids. Once you know who you're looking for, never stop your search for that next pair of hands.

> *Busy teams are happy teams. And happy teams are profitable teams.*

If you stop looking to hire because you don't have enough consistent, loyal clients to keep that new person busy, then you're missing the point. Go out and get those clients! Look for clients and staff at the same time, continuously. If you have more clients and not enough people on your team, then demand is high and you can revisit your price point. Again, I applaud you. The other way around just isn't workable – team members standing around idle is not a good look, either in your salon or in your profit and loss figures.

When I see a café that's brimming with people, I'm happy to queue up to get in. I know it must have great food and service and that the wait will be worthwhile. Like most people, I don't queue for places where the food and service are crap. If I have a choice between a café that's completely empty and lining up next-door at a café that's full and vibrant, I'll choose the queue any day.

Have you ever heard the term "water attracts water"? Water, from any direction, will always find its way to other water as it flows toward the lowest point. It's gravity and it's what creates our vast oceans. People are the same – in salons, pubs, cafés and bookstores, they're drawn to other people, only it's not gravity that unites them, it's the quality of the experience. Take busking for example. Whenever there's a big crowd around a busker, I'm instantly drawn to see what's going on. A big crowd tells me it must be good! Keep that in mind when you're having a quiet patch in your salon. Have team members pair-up to put bums on seats as they fiddle with one another's hair. It's not only good practice, but the next potential client walking past doesn't know they both work there and will be less likely to judge your business negatively by the number of clients they can see.

Whatever you do, never drop the ball on growing, whether it's the size of your client base or the size of your team. Keep your team occupied and productive. Busy teams are happy teams. And happy teams are profitable teams.

The Nitty Gritty.

Keep on moving, keep on improving, keep on growing.

Think about extending your open hours.

Think about bigger premises.

Never stop marketing for new clients.

Never stop looking for new team members.

chapter 5

5

Safety in numbers.

My first apprentice walked in my salon door and I offered her a job because – if I'm really honest – she was beautifully presented. She'd just finished Year 12 and wanted to be a hairdresser, despite her parents doing their best to talk her out of it. That was a Thursday night, it was pouring with rain and I remember it like it was yesterday. Up until then, I was a one-woman show. She was employed over the weekend and started the following Monday.

I was desperate for another pair of hands. I let her do everything I was doing from the first day she arrived. Fifteen months later, she'd finished all her schooling and could do everything I could do. She had a great teacher in me and I gave her all of my attention. We were a match made in heaven. I've not met another one like her.

Her walking in was an absolute fluke. At least that's what I thought, at first. Except that I later discovered the real estate agent had told her mother to send her daughter in to see me because she thought I was an awesome businesswoman with a great way with people. She said if I was hiring, she'd be sending her own kid there. Although I hadn't advertised, without realising it I was putting it out there. People see your true talents even if you don't.

One of the things that draws a person to our industry in the first place is that they like people. Naturally, they're going to be drawn to salon owners and teams where they see like-minded people – people who create an environment where they feel they'll belong.

Apart from the odd I-hate-the-whole-world-type person, I can say one of the things I have enjoyed most about the hair and beauty community is their ability to connect with other people. They seem to be the happiest when they're amongst people – all kinds of people, the good, the bad, and the not-so-good and worse (you know: the dickheads). We still enjoy them, too. It's all part of what makes our salon day entertaining.

What's really tough is when you're a single operator and you're advertising for your very first team member. More often than not, this will put you at a disadvantage. The bigger your team, the easier it is to attract staff. From the very beginning, we're team players. That doesn't mean we're necessarily good at it, but we do like to surround ourselves with people. Until you get above five team members you'll find it more difficult.

From the employee point of view, when they're the only person on the team, it makes it more difficult for them to schedule holidays, knowing they leave such a large gap if they're absent for any reason. If there are eight or more on team, they always know there are others to help out when they're not available. When there are only two people on your team, it's more challenging to keep up momentum and energy, and the chances of you getting into a creative rut are a little higher. I always loved it when a new senior would come into our team because they always brought fresh ideas, new ways to do things. The fresh energy can really fire up an already great mix.

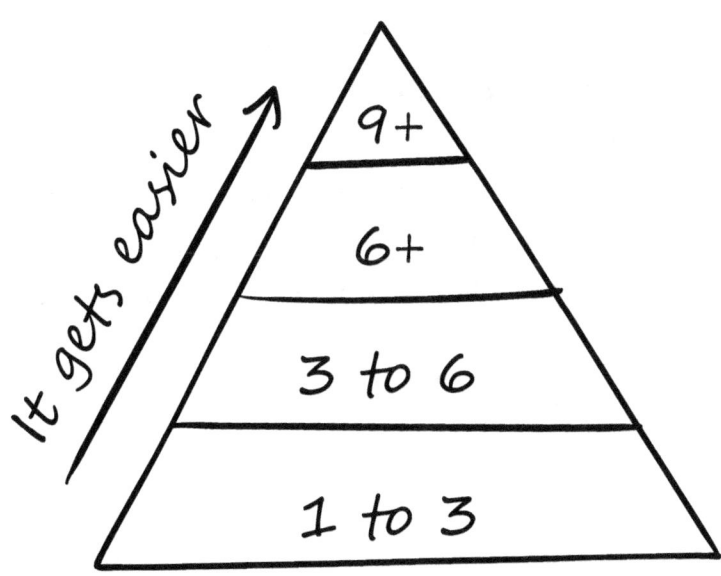

When you're a team of one or two, you can't help but draw all the focus and attention. While focus can be a great thing, in this case, it means you're only going to learn one way of doing things. An awesome teacher can still bring in fresh ideas to the mix but it's a challenge not everyone's up to. This one-size learning can be a lot more pressure than many of you'd prefer.

> *People see your true talents even if you don't.*

From a business point of view, if you can manage a team of two you should be able to manage a team of twelve. In many ways, it's easier because. A large team demands a lot of juggling but can also spread training, issues and problems across a broader base with a really cohesive team supporting one another and allowing you to be a little more removed. And, that has to be a good thing!

The Nitty Gritty.

Most people in our industry are "people" people.

They're drawn to like-minded people.

The bigger your team, the easier it is to attract great people.

chapter 6

Hiring who you need, when you need (it's about mandarins and oranges).

When I started out as a hairdresser, I got my best break ever when another girl in our salon team fell pregnant. While everyone was excited about the baby, I was more excited that her salon clients would need someone to look after them. I wanted to be that someone.

I hatched a plan to go out of my way to schmooze the mum-to-be's clients. I wanted to be noticed and front of mind when the time came for the big question: *Who do you want me to book you in with next time, when I'm maternity leave?*

Many of those clients replied along the lines of: *What about the friendly new girl, Lisa?* Bingo! I was in and I never looked back. It had nothing to do with commissions or targets. For me, it was all about wanting to do the job and be the awesome hairdresser I knew I could be. If my boss had hired a new fully qualified stylist to fill the maternity leave gap, I might still be tied to that basin and broom.

As a salon owner, you already know that it's rare for things to just fall into place like they did for me and my boss (albeit with a bit of a nudge).

So, unless you have a gap caused by a team member going on leave, or actually leaving to go elsewhere, how do you know when the time is right to add to you team? It's not guesswork and it's not rocket science. It's all to do with your figures. ***Everything*** is to do with your figures.

If your whole team is fully booked 75% or more in advance, then the time is right. In simple terms, that figure means seven out of every ten of your clients are rebooking. Congratulations, that's an amazing accomplishment in itself. It's natural that up to 25% of your client base will have trouble committing to their next appointment time. Shift workers, unorganised people or those who travel frequently for work make up a big chunk of this group. They're more likely to walk in off the street or call up at a day's notice. I call them salon nomads or the "great untrained".

Training these clients to rebook is your first step. I personally trained hundreds of them over the years. Sometimes I felt like Steve Irwin wrestling a crocodile as I tried to get them to commit to their next appointment. Usually my mantra – *if you want me, you have to book* – got them across the line and into the appointment book. They got the message that, like a great restaurant, doctor or exclusive private school, I'm a limited resource and if you don't book a spot you don't get one.

If you take the time to ~~wrestle~~ train your clients and your rebooking rate hits 75%, then you should seriously look at adding another person to your already great team.

> **It's not guesswork and it's not rocket science. It's all to do with your figures.**

Another handy way to measure is to keep a notebook beside the reception desk where you jot down the names of people who made enquiries for a spot but couldn't be accommodated. Only include people who you know you would love to look after. Don't confuse this list with the "fish list" also known as the "ones that John West rejects". You know who I mean, the ones who start the conversation with *How much does it cost?* and finish off with *But I need it today!*

It depends on the size of the salon, but by general rule of thumb, if one person on your team is knocking back two or more people a day, you need more feet on the floor.

> **Do NOT hire an ex beauty therapist or hairdresser as your receptionist.**

Before you rush out and place a job ad, have a long hard look at who is coming up the ladder. Your next qualified team member could be right under your nose, waiting in the wings for their chance to shine. Remember the story I told you about my big break? Who else do you have coming up the ranks? Maybe a great third-year apprentice or someone in your beauty ranks who can already do three quarters of the beauty treatments you offer and deserves a chance to step-up.

As a salon owner, I learnt early that training from within the team gave me far more joy than trying to retrain someone from some other salon. I never did find a new, qualified person who just slotted straight in. They always needed a good hard polish. I called them "plasticine" because they needed a remoulding in one way or another. Sometimes in a big way.

The bottom line is how much potential you see in each prospective team member. If you find someone you want to keep or hire into your salon who is keen to be trained, then for goodness sake, train them and train them fast! There is no better place to start. If you're upfront and truthful when looking for new additions, you'll actually grow wings in your business. It has to be a two-way thing.

Do you need a junior, a senior or a superstar support person?

Staffing is like a game of chess. You need to be constantly looking at your team, seeing what pieces you have, predicting the shifts ahead and working out your next move. What do you really need to take the next step in your salon? Is it a senior? Is it a junior? A salon coordinator, an assistant or even a receptionist? Or do you yearn for someone to do the ironing and collect the kids from school? A great salon owner is always – always! – thinking about who or what the next team member needs to be.

It's a tough climate and finding staff has never been more difficult. You need to think outside the box to get the right resources into your team. Lots are turning to other support in the salon, rather than just growing the floor team. By this I mean receptionists and salon coordinators as well as basin team members.

Your Salon Team

In an ideal world, every single one of you would have a receptionist. Having a receptionist on board elevates your salon to a whole new level. I'm shocked that some salons have a very high price point, yet allow their team members to be pulled away to answer the phone. Sorry, but that's not high-end service. Or in beauty, when every phone call goes to message bank over and over again and you lock the salon door when you're doing a treatment. I get that you can't leave a Brazilian wax half-way through, but ignoring your incoming calls or clients knocking on your door is just the worst thing to do in business. I've moved on from more than one beauty salon for that exact reason. I'm a good spender, I love paying for anything that makes me look and feel better, but I expect and deserve better from a professional salon.

Work out how you can afford a receptionist and get one.

Trust me, you won't regret it. Teach them the ins and outs of the salon then watch them manage it all while you get on with more important tasks. They can tell you every move in the appointment book. They can book people in correctly without those wasteful 15-minute gaps. They can follow-up visits with a courtesy call, confirm appointments, allow time for basin services, explain where clients can park, outline this month's promotion, order stock as well as do the wages, rosters and marketing. I call the really good ones the "work wife". I know – not politically correct, but it's fitting.

If you're sold on the idea of a receptionist, I have an insider tip for you. Do NOT hire an ex beauty therapist or hairdresser as your receptionist. The best front desk people use a different side of their brain. It's not a creative right brain; it's the opposite, the left side. It's much better at the task and the detail. They get the job done without the fluffing about. We creative brains seem to overcomplicate things with the emotional stuff. You want your receptionist to make decisions based on fact and without getting swept up by the salon BS.

Better still, if they haven't had a career in the industry, they won't start their sentences with *in my salon* ... and they won't suffer from the know-it-all syndrome. Instead, they'll take your instructions and direction to the letter and you can expect a fresh air of calmness to waft through your salon.

So, work it into your plan. Get yourself a PA, receptionist or coordinator – call them whatever you like. A true salon support person is what you need to lift your business to a whole new level of service. Your entire team and your clients will love you for it.

Mandarins and oranges (getting what you want in your new team member).

What have mandarins and oranges got to do with it? I know that people, like fruit, are often nothing like what they seem. They're like mandarins and oranges – on the outside, a large mandarin and a small orange look very similar. But have you ever tried peeling and eating an orange while driving a car? Yes? Then you know they are two very different fruits. Ever tried juicing a mandarin? Again, two very different fruits. Same colour, same exterior but miles apart when you come to use them. Same but different.

Prospective salon team members are like mandarins and oranges. They can all look similar at first glance, but when you peel back the layers in the salon environment you might be surprised what you find.

How do you get what you want in the next person you invite to join your team? I find that salon owners rarely make a list of the qualities they're seeking when hiring. Instead, they cross their fingers and hope that someone "good" comes along and

> **I know that *people*, like *fruit*, are often nothing like what they seem.**

falls in their lap. Like everything in life, if you have a clear understanding of what you're seeking, you're much more likely to find it.

Too often, salon owners frame their job ads around a particular skill level, rather than a particular personality or mindset.

Flip that thinking on its head, and you just might have a blueprint for getting what you really want and need in one fabulous new team member.

Consider this analogy. When you visit the optometrist and you're choosing your new glasses, you're usually asked to scan over walls and walls of frames arranged according to various company and designer brands, or perhaps price points. You end up trying on dozens of pairs and most of them are totally wrong for you. How overwhelming and inefficient is that process? Imagine, instead, if your first stop was a face shape guide, perhaps even a short YouTube tutorial about learning your face shape? Once you understand your face shape you move on to the relevant section. There could be a section of frames suited to round faces. Another suited to heart-shaped faces. And so on. There could even be examples of famous face shapes. Demi Moore could be poster girl for the classic square-shaped face and Cameron Diaz for the round-shaped. How much easier would it be for you? You'd know what you were looking for – it's clearly mapped out for you.

So, instead of wandering in to your hiring process unprepared (as you do at most optometrists) you need a list of the qualities you know you enjoy in staff members and co-workers. You need to understand what you're looking for. Grab a notebook and half an hour, sit down and think back over your years in the industry. Think about the people you've worked with or under, the people you've managed or led, the people you've lunched with in the backroom, the people who've trained you and even the people who've actually done your hair or beauty services for you. Now, as you think through those people, list down the qualities you love about them, what drew you to them, what you admired in their work or their manner.

Now, look that list over carefully ... because that's your hiring list – a checklist of the qualities you're seeking in your next team member.

Here's something else for you to consider.

It's a mistake I often see salon owners make. Perhaps it's your mistake, too? You narrow down your people search by using a number. You feel compelled to quantify the job requirements, especially when it comes to experience. Like this for example:

A senior colourist with a minimum of five years' experience.

Does that mean if I've got only two years' experience, even though I'd love to work in your business and I'm genuinely passionate and a model team member, I shouldn't apply? What you're really doing by narrowing down your search in this way is blocking certain people from throwing their hat into the ring. And have you thought that you might attract someone with 10 years' experience who is so out of touch and set in their ways that there's no way they'd fit into your salon culture?

There just aren't enough quality people applying for the available positions in hair and beauty. If you want to attract the best there is, you need to think outside the box. (See Chapter 7 on writing your job ad for more tips.)

In my salon, I'd much prefer someone who's less skilled but ready and keen to learn, someone who needs me to invest time and energy to bring out the best in them and get them to a standard we can both be proud of.

The secret here is that we both want things from this working relationship – neither of us is doing the other a favour. And that's the basis of a great relationship (professional or personal). They will grow into my salon's culture, understand my values, get my principles, embrace the way we deliver our client care and be part of my salon's point of difference from the ground up. Sure, in the early days, they may not be at a skill level I want but it's so much easier – a pleasure, even – to teach someone who wants to learn.

That's what I call a win win. Like when you're driving down the highway and you reach into your bag and heave a sigh of relief that you packed a mandarin and not an orange.

The Nitty Gritty.

Check your figures to know when the time is right to hire.

See who's already waiting in the wings.

Always be planning your next staffing move.

Think about what and who you really need.

People are often not what they seem.

Make a hiring checklist of the people qualities you love.

Don't use your job ad to narrow your search.

Be prepared to invest time and effort to train your new team member.

chapter 7

7

Where to advertise and how to write a winning job ad.

I once had a man phone me about a job advertisement for my salon. He'd clipped the ad from the local paper, stuck it on the fridge and eventually made the call himself. Nothing unusual there … except that he was enquiring on behalf of his wife. She was unhappy in her current salon, barely tolerating her boss and had worked for a string of salon owners who didn't seem to value what she did. Her gorgeous husband had seized the opportunity and taken it upon himself to help her move on to somewhere she'd be happier.

My point is: you never know who's seeing or reading your job ad, or what their connections might be. You might laugh to think I placed my ad in the local newspaper. Not such a sophisticated choice, you say? Who reads that paper anyway? The fact is: the right ad can be powerful in any medium and sometimes it's worth throwing your net wide and far. (At the end of the chapter, I'll share the wording of that ad I placed in the local paper and you'll understand why husband-of-the-year made that call.)

So, where should you advertise for people to join your salon team? The short answer is anywhere typical hairdressers or beauty therapists gather or interact, either in real life or in the digital world. Where are their campfires? Where do they chat and network, learn and shop, socialise and hang-out?

Think about: salon suppliers, training colleges, Facebook, Instagram, any other social media you use. Don't forget your website and local noticeboards.

> *the right ad can be powerful in any medium*

I find many salon owners resistant to using a wide range of options for advertising. They say they simply want to identify the medium that will get them the right person. It's the kind of lazy thinking that's holding them back because there is no right answer – what's effective today might not be tomorrow or next week.

What about your salon window or A-frame board? It's right near where people slow down to push open your salon door. Don't start on me. This notion seems to raise most salon owners' eyebrows. *What, you mean on my salon door? Nope, that looks cheap.* My response is clear: it only looks cheap if you create a cheap ad.

Some salon owners are hell-bent on telling me why something isn't going to work. I figure if they had it all sorted, they wouldn't be needing me or be asking for my advice. From time to time, I remind them of that fact.

If you're going to be "head of the prevention department" – or as my mother used to point out, "leader of the opposition" – you'll oppose everything new, no matter what I suggest. And you'll ruffle my feathers big time. I'll tell you that I'd love to hear your plan. You'll tell me you don't have one. I'll say: "exactly!" Because either you don't have a plan or you have one that isn't delivering the results you want.

Back to your ad at your salon door. Why not elevate it from cheap to luxe-looking with a little fiddling in your favourite computer photo editing software or app? You could create a professional-looking ad by including a stylish image of a great haircut or fabulous makeup, perhaps along with a snap of your salon team, all looking polished, happy and inviting. Try printing it out on photo-quality paper or ask at your local print shop about an A3-sized print.

Your ad might say:

> Our business is having a growth spurt and we need more of us to look after our lovely, loyal clients. Apply within.

OR

> If this is the quality of work you'd love to do, then we are looking for you. We need another awesome person to join our beauty family. We have a rare opportunity available for the right person. If that's you, please leave your CV at reception and we'll be in touch.

Nothing cheap about that. It's positive, conveys the success of your business and is great for your salon's brand. So, dump that lazy thinking. Look around you for the many opportunities to reach out to the wider world with your job advertisement. You won't know what's out there until you give it a red-hot go.

Now, about my advert in the local paper that attracted my new team member's husband. It simply read:

> Hairdressers: if you're tired of working hard for little or no reward and would much rather be appreciated for your years of industry dedication, then let's meet.

How to write a winning job ad.

Think back to a time before you owned a salon, when you worked for a team, rather than leading it. When you found yourself on the hunt for a fulfilling role in another salon, how did you decide where to apply? What was it about a job vacancy advertisement that caught your eye and peeked your interest, sometimes when you weren't even seriously looking?

Stay in that mindset because the looking-for-a-great-job you is exactly the person you need to envision when you're writing your next job ad for your own salon. Think about how the wording of your job ad can work extra hard to attract and win awesome people (just like you) to your team.

I shake my head in disbelief at some of the job ads I read online on sites like seek.com. They're mostly boring and bland. Invariably, they start with the must-haves.

> **POSITION AVAILABLE**
>
> Must have five years' experience, be enthusiastic. Must be well-presented and must be proficient in all aspects of hairdressing. People who are new to our industry need not apply. We are only interested in someone who can cut and colour hair.

Reading this, I'd be scared to ask if I could go to the bathroom! How beige is it? There's no colour or life. Why would anyone want to work there?

Flip it on its head. Instead of focusing on what your new team member must have, try highlighting what they'll find in your salon and how they'll feel as part of your superb team. Start with what your audience knows to be true. Connect with them in the first line, address their pain points and pander to their likely wish list for their new role.

A SALON TEAM WORTH JOINING

What you'll find at XXXXXX Hair and Beauty, is that you're appreciated for the work you do. Being an engaged stylist is no easy feat. In our salon environment, you'll find other like-minded and passionate people. You won't have to explain your love and passion here; we get it. The owner (that's me) loves what she does, too.

We're happy to wait for the right person. Our client base is growing and you might be just the right fit for our team. So we (you and I both) can work that out, let's meet up for an informal chat. Of course, your enquiry will be totally confidential. We'd expect you to be able to manage day-to-day cut and colour challenges, but you'll have our team's support 100% in the beginning, while you're finding your feet, and every day after that, as we are a hair family.

Let's talk: XXXX XXX XXX (Rebecca)

What do you think? Can you see that they both ask for the same thing only one sounds tired and grumpy, and the other sounds realistic and positive? I know which team I'd rather join. What about you?

Keep the wheels rolling.

You have two wheels to roll: finding clients and finding staff. You need to roll both at the same time. Always. Constantly. You can't drop the ball on either.

It frightens me that some salon owners are stuck. They're so set in their ways; they're in a holding pattern for years, stuck on a team of two or four.

They don't have enough clients (regular, consistent clients, that is) so they can't add to the team size. They get stuck so deep in a salon rut that they start believing there aren't any people out there to even answer their boring, lacklustre advertisement.

Here's the thing: most salons don't find their people through Seek. They find them by being part of a much bigger community based on word of mouth. They get out and about. See Chapter 3 *Google, gather and go.* for my tips. And get your ad written up to reflect your mindset. You'll be surprised what happens.

I have salons on my books that can always find the right people. They expect they will, they believe they can and they're right.

> *You have two wheels to roll: finding clients and finding staff. You need to roll both at the same time. Always. Constantly.*

Isn't that interesting? They're rocking business in all sorts of ways and they're getting noticed by others in the industry – peers, competitors, and stylists and therapists in other salons.

When you have this vibe going on, some of those people start thinking about joining your team. They might wander in and leave a CV, stalk your Facebook and Instagram, or drive past your salon to check how busy you are. They ask around and people encourage them to go in. And they do.

The bad news: there's no "fake it until you make it" when it comes to that salon vibe. You have to pull on that t-shirt I mention in my book *The Naked Salon* and work harder on yourself than on any one else. Then, and only then, will you rise to be this awesome boss … and an employer of choice.

Get ahead of the game with a Plan B for hiring.

Consider advertising for team members even when you're not really looking. Have you ever been shopping for shoes and come home with a dress? That's what happens. It's the same with people making career moves – sometimes, they don't know what they want until they see an opportunity.

Always be on the look-out because, at any stage, one of your team could be about to move on. *I'm pregnant. I want to work in real estate. I'm going to back-pack around Europe for a year.* You know the conversations and you know they can come out of the blue. So, always be ready with a Plan B and you'll have the options you need to keep your salon team rolling along on all wheels.

The Nitty Gritty.

Cast your net far and wide.

Advertise where your industry tribe gathers.

Try an ad at your salon door.

Get creative and make it visually inviting.

Who do you want to attract to your team?
Write your ad for them.

Make it inviting and emotional. Tell them how your salon feels.

Be always seeking clients and staff.

Find great people through your industry networks.

Attract the best with your awesome salon vibe.

chapter 8

8

Passion versus skill: going deep during the interview and those first few weeks.

One day, way back on the farm in Hopetoun, I can remember my dad showing me how to mix up the horse feed in the stables. I didn't enjoy much about horses but Dad needed my help. He pointed out that the dollar value of the six or so horses we were feeding spanned a big range. A couple of them weren't worth much at all but one in particular was worth a bundle. Despite the figures, the horses' owners each valued their own horse and to Dad, they all deserved the same exceptional care. "Their money is all the same," he said. "Fifty dollars is fifty dollars." He never took any horse's dollar value into consideration when he made up the feeds because his passion for what he did meant that every animal in his charge enjoyed the best possible care he could provide. No compromises. That day, Dad's passion shone through and I've carried the learnings with me ever since.

The big question for salon owners and their team is: *What's more important – passion or skill?*

I often see great people overlooked for salon positions because they don't have the required skill to fill that narrow hole the salon owner thinks needs plugging up. I made this mistake myself, many times over, before I realised that passion and skill actually come in that order.

You can have a natural skill but if it doesn't float your boat, you're just going through the motions. For example, I reckon I'm a great mentor and you might think that means I could translate my skills to other industries beyond hair and beauty. Really? I think not. My passion lies in this one. Maybe I could coach clothing store owners, because that's another sector driven by personal appearance, but there's no way I could look after a plumber or an electrician. Sure, like salon owners, those tradies would have an average dollar sale and a break even point and they'd need a plan. It's just not my sweetspot.

Your level of passion determines your perseverance and tolerance to push through when you're not getting the results you want. Without passion, you'll give up at the first sign of struggle, and that's not the type of team member you want to be saddled with.

So, when it comes to finding that ideal person to join your salon team, how can you assess their level of passion? You don't know them well and you might have only one or two interview opportunities to discover more about them.

The trouble is that people throw the word "passion" around like it's going out of style. It's simple for an interviewee to tell you that hairdressing or beauty is their passion. I suggest you take it with a grain of salt and every time you hear that word in a job interview, re-hear it in your head as *blah, blah, blah*, because that's all it's really worth. They'll tell you almost anything to impress you at an interview.

I'm going to teach you how to fish around, to dig deeper using better questions to flush out better answers. You'll be clued up with a much clearer understanding of whether the person in front of you truly does have the level of professional passion you're looking for.

I've created a resource to help you. Go to: **www.yoursalonteam.com.au/resources** and download my Sample Interview Questions sheet. Each of these questions relates directly back to better understanding the level of passion for whoever you're interviewing.

I won't bore you here with a run-down of each question. Go have a look for yourself and you'll get where I'm coming from.

But I do want to emphasise one question theme I can't recommend highly enough. *What motivates you to do this work?*

Where is the buzz in it for you? At what moment do you say, "Yes, that's the reason I do what I do?"

For me, in my work as a mentor, it's when I get a random text from a coaching client saying, "For the first time in 10 years, I've just paid my BAS in full because the money was sitting in an offset account! My accountant says he's never been more proud of me." Right there, I know they've developed good business practices and that someone other than myself is impressed.

When you ask that question at an interview, there are things to look for: a sense of feeling or emotion that goes deeper than the word passion. It might go something like this:

I love it when someone comes in for just a trim and I know that if I ask the right questions I can turn that simple trim request into much more than just a haircut."

or

By exploring a much wider horizon or bigger picture that may include colour or basin services and the right products to support what we've just created for them, that's where I get my buzz. Right there.

or

Coming across a client who doesn't know what's available to them, so I take their skin from where it is today to having a glow about it. People don't know what's available and I love educating them because 9 out of 10 of them are so grateful for my knowledge.

or

Being open and honest about what's possible, steering people around what won't work for them and steering them to what I know will work. That gives me a joy.

or

Drawing up a plan for someone's skin, setting up the samples and delivering knowledge and service in a package that just flows out of me and into them.

or

I get a buzz from solving people's problems with products. Most of them are confused and don't know where to start, so I break it down and simplify it so they feel like I'm the solution for what they want to achieve, like an interpreter. Then, when they return and thank me, I get excited. Once they realise there's so much more they can be doing for their appearance, they're thrilled and so am I.

Any of these responses would be music to my ears. They strongly reflect how I feel about what I do.

This kind of thinking was just in my DNA. I'm certain it stems from my father. Remember my horse story? I've always felt that our clients should each receive the same exceptional care and I made sure my team understood this thinking, too. I can recall a boss saying "I've booked in 'such and such' – make sure you look after her." I found this offensive because I treated everyone equally well.

Having passion about what you do means you can more easily roll with the ups and downs of day-to-day salon life. You don't let mood swings or personal dramas get in the way of delivering an awesome experience for every client, every day. Because you're driven by the client outcome, not the process or the money or the status.

> **Because you're *driven by* the *client outcome*, not the process or the money or the status.**

Let me tell you a story – it's a cautionary tale about inviting someone without passion to join your salon team.

Leanne worked for me for only for a few months before I figured her out. It was a long few months! Leanne could cut hair technically better than me. Way better. What an awesome thing that could have been, if not for her moods.

On a good day, Leanne had a pleasant enough personality. On a bad day, she barely spoke to her clients not even for a tea or coffee order. I don't get how she thought she could manage a consultation without speaking. No matter her mood, her skill level was never compromised. Failing putting witches hats around her chair to warn clients when she was having a

bad day, I was at my wit's end. I had no idea what version of Leanne might appear on any given day. At times, Leanne even admitted to being a bitch. She knew her shortcomings, but felt unable to do anything about it. *That's just me. I'm a proper bitch, and it doesn't really bother me.* In the end, we parted ways because I couldn't keep taking myself and the rest of the team along for the ride on her emotional rollercoaster.

It's a shame and such a waste of Leanne's skills. And, I'm certain she's still a bitch. Her stinking attitude will still be hanging around, wherever she is (or isn't) working today.

I remember how her negative stink would waft through the salon, like that stinky odour you smell in your fridge. The one that gets up your nose whenever you open the door. You keep looking to see where it comes from. In your fridge, it's nearly always something in the crisper, right at the back where it's not easy to see. You have to search for it. It's the same in the salon … and it's nearly always a team member who lacks the passion to push herself through a mood swing or a not-so-great day. In your salon, a stinky smell like that is constantly distracting for you, your team and your clients.

Think about that stinky smell when you're next hiring. If you're aware, it will tease at your nose and tug at your gut instinct during the interview. You don't have to settle for someone who isn't right for your salon. Instead, go the extra mile and ask those deep-diving questions to sniff out the real professional passion.

Nine days. Nine weeks. Nine months.

I wish there was a diagnosis kit available, something similar to a pregnancy test that you could use when hiring staff. How cool would it be, if you could simply ask for a urine sample from a possible team member to test and find out if they have the qualities – and the passion – you're looking for? It could come back green for a big YES and red for a definite NO.

OK, OK, enough with the dreaming, already. In the absence of a diagnostic dipping stick, let's look at your options.

We all employ staff we wish we hadn't. It's as though the person who shows up for the interview is not the same person you end up working side-by-side with a few weeks later. Most people put their best foot forward during an interview and also during the trade test. Some people are just not who they present to be and it's our job to work that out as fast as we can.

My experience is that when we all start to work with a new team member, we're still looking for things to appear. That's really the only way that we can find out for sure – put them into our business and work with them for a period of time.

I've noticed that most salon owners have had very little practice in picking up the warning signs, even though they're always obvious in hindsight. The average time it takes to work out if a person is suitable or not is nine months. For some reason, that's just the time it seems to take.

An experienced salon owner, who has changed over many team members and been around in the industry for a few years, would only take about nine weeks to evaluate a new team member. That's great timing – just before the three-month probation period ends.

Then there's someone like me, who can tell you in just nine days (less, if I'm being really honest). There has to be some benefits to getting older, guys! Give me something, please.

Think about this: the longer you procrastinate and can't decide whether this person is or isn't suitable, the higher the risk is to your business. If they're not suitable in the end, they have been in contact with more of your clients than you'd prefer. The wrong person being a part of your team can do much damage to your business in nine months.

On the other hand, nine weeks is just a tad over two months. Most of your clients will have only met this person once in that time.

Knowing they're not right in nine days means most of your clientele won't have met them at all. If they're a rotten apple, the least amount of time they have in touch with your clients and your team, the better.

So, watch them like a hawk, test their work and ring your clients to get feedback. Talk to your team members about how they feel around the new person and really do your homework, so you're closer to the nine days than nine months.

Take off those rose-coloured glasses. Keep them for when you look at your family (the ones you *have* to keep). Evaluate, be honest with yourself and be prepared to make a decision early.

The Nitty Gritty.

Passion comes before skills.

Download Sample Interview Questions to help you identify passion.

Look for emotion in the answers.

Don't settle for someone with no professional passion. They stink.

When you get a new team member, watch them carefully.

Keep assessing whether they're right for your salon.

Reduce the risk to your business by deciding earlier rather than later.

chapter 9

9

When your salon's a family affair.

There's an old showbiz adage that you should never work with kids or animals. In the salon, I think you could almost add "your family" to the list. Just to remind you that working with family can go either way. Careful. There are some tricky bits.

Of course, if you're convinced that your wife, your cousin, your brother or your giddy aunt is the right person for the job, then go ahead. Carefully. There are some tricky bits.

I see some salon staff who'd be marched out the door so fast their head would spin if they weren't related to the owner. Family tend to expect extra privileges and less responsibility. As the salon owner, you tend to be more tolerant of their shortcomings and more likely to give them a second chance. Or even a third or fourth chance. I've heard people describe fellow team members who are related to the owner as having "more lives than an alley cat". In case you don't know, that's more than nine lives.

Still, if someone in your family is a solid operator, is good for your business and you're confident they'll add value for your team and your clients, welcome them and treasure them.

Of course, it's not all bad. Family don't generally run off at the first sign of trouble and can be more loyal than your average employee. Just remember: lines are easily blurred when it comes to family members and it could all end in tears. Christmas lunch could be ugly. You need to proceed with caution.

You need to put clear boundaries in place.

If you happen to live with your co-working family member, at the end of the day, you need to leave work matters at the salon. It will be a challenge. Near impossible, in fact. So, before you ask partner, daughter or live-in family member an after-hours work question, ask yourself: *Can this wait?* If it can't wait, if you'll sleep better, be able to finish the payroll or it makes you understand that note in the day's takings, then go ahead. Those fall under the *Fire and Blood Rule*.

If there's fire or you might even smell smoke (that's the *Smoke Rule*) or you get the feeling you'll be needing a band aid anytime soon – *Blood Rule* – it's important. But, rather than blurting out, "What the hell happened today X, Y and Z?" while your loved one is sinking into a G&T on the balcony is not on. You need to say, "When is a good time? I have a couple of questions I need to ask." You need to respect each other's work life balance. I'll repeat: EACH OTHER'S – my experience is you are both guilty of the blur.

If you have a big idea that needs to be talked through, take it "offshore". By offshore, I mean to a place other than your home: go out for a walk, a coffee or a wine. Home should be where you're happiest, filled with the people you love and the things you have collected over your lifetime.

> *Family tend to expect extra privileges and less responsibility.*

I think it was Billy Connolly who likened his bed to a lighthouse. It was like a nest, the thing he focused on making it back to, just like a bird might. Every night when he climbed into bed, he was drawn, as if by a lighthouse, to the prize: white sheets, a book waiting where he'd left off and surrounded by family photos. The last thing you'd want to bring into that peaceful scenario is the troubles from your salon. Keep business strictly out of your pillow talk.

Family members need to be team members (not family members) during working hours. It can be tricky to separate the two.

A salon owner (a coaching client) recently told me his wife was meant to be doing a particular task at the salon, something that really needed to be done. When it wasn't done and I quizzed him about it, he replied that his wife gets bogged down with dropping off and picking up the kids. Note, the kids are 14 and 16 years of age, so no one needs a nappy change! I asked if his wife was on a normal hourly rate like the rest of his team, would he be happy with her running her children everywhere on salon time. He said: "If not for the fact they're my kids, I'd eff-ing sack her!" We both roared laughing. But he knew what needed to be done. "You can tell her," he said. "I've had my head bitten off more than once for mentioning it."

> **We all want a voice, but it can be hard to find a place to be heard when family dynamics merge into the workplace.**

See how hard it can be? The truth is: the way we show up is everything. That isn't any way to run a business. If she worked for anyone else, she'd get those kids into a car pool or insist they walk or ride to and from school. My twin boys were always trying to get me to collect them from soccer training. They'd say, "You're the boss, can't you just leave?" My answer was always the same, "You're young, fit and healthy boys with two good legs. Walk home. I've got a job to do and it's important to me that I lead by example. And when you get home, don't leave the toaster on the bench!"

It's all about respect.

All businesses need a good sense of balance. You need to rely on, trust and respect those you work with and family is no different. I notice that family members working together in salons often speak poorly to one another. You would never speak to paid team members harshly, so don't speak to family that way. Everyone deserves the same respect – employees, employers, blood family or work family. Same same.

Breaking up is hard to do.

Most businesses start off like a marriage – everyone's excited and gets carried away with the idea. But no one's given any thought to how the business will end. *Will it be sold? Will someone want to move on and another want to stay?*

Like any relationship, it's way more fun going in than it is coming out. That's probably the biggest understatement ever! It can be so painful coming out that you swear you'll never do it again. Ever! Most end up with a severe case of the double Bs – *Burnt and Bitter*. I think there's a T-shirt that people could wear so you don't have to guess. It's got a big BB on the front for "Burnt and Bitter" not "Big Boobs".

In a business, especially in a salon, it's not "until death we do part" – eventually it has to be sold, shut down or passed on to someone else. Try passing down a marriage to someone when you die.

In business, most of the parting is done long before death. It's something you need to consider because in a family business it's way more complicated. The passing on or passing over (or whatever you might call it) is where a lot of trouble starts.

I think it's because family members naturally assume they're going to get the business handed to them. Sometimes, it's parents assuming their children actually *want* the business. What this needs is some open communication so everyone knows where they stand. Gather the family troops around without any distractions and have a serious discussion. Give everyone five minutes uninterrupted to have their say. Make the topic: *In 5 years I want to be ...* or adjust it to suit where your family is at. Together you can stop assuming and start talking and planning for a future that works for everyone.

I see an amazing level of assumption going on in family businesses. Often I'm asked as the business coach to be the one who asks the hard questions and gets the conversations happening. We all want a voice, but it can be hard to find a place to be heard when family dynamics merge into the workplace. It becomes even more complicated when there are more than two family members working in a business.

What happens when one family member wants to sell their share or go do something else with their career and another one wants to stay? You can imagine how uncomfortable those conversations are! I suggest you have an agreement that every 12 months, on the anniversary of when you opened the door, you'll all sit down together and agree on a plan for the next 12 months, putting in place any necessary conditions or expectations. That way, everyone has the opportunity to have their say. And, if someone doesn't want to stay, they have a chance to say so.

I love working with families – they're challenging because there are so many layers. What's refreshing is that they're always grateful for a fresh set of eyes. It's one of my biggest challenges as a business coach, yet one of the most rewarding and satisfying when things are resolved and people feel heard, respected and more certain about the future.

The Nitty Gritty.

Be warned, working with family is tricky.

Think carefully if they're the best fit for your salon.

Set clear boundaries.

Strive for mutual respect.

Open lines of communication.

Plan for a way out in the future.

chapter 10

10

The miracle of motivation and upping an attitude score.

The other morning I jumped on a tram and noticed a girl with bright red hair seated nearby. We caught each other's eye and realised we knew each other. Let's call her Ruby. She was from a salon where I used to pop in to have my threading done, though I never had my hair done there. I asked her how things were going and she said she was now qualified. "Fantastic!" I said. "Except I've been put to part-time," she said. Ruby's a mum with a couple of kids and she'd been a mature age apprentice. It saddened me that her hours had been cut and I wondered why her boss had done that. "Did you do all your training with the one boss?" I asked. She had. A few more questions and I figured out there were holes on both sides of this tale.

Ruby is a pleasant kid. I've watched her with clients in the salon and she's great. I think what's happened along the way is that the system lets us down and some salon owners don't understand what their job is. Your job is to make sure that when your apprentice (like Ruby) qualifies, she has a full clientele so you don't have to make her part-time.

Ruby is dedicated to her job. The Saturday I saw her, she was tramming it all the way in from an outer suburb to get to work on time. But her hair looked terrible. Her makeup looked terrible. Apart from her bright red hair, there's no way I'd have picked her as part of the hair and beauty industry.

> *Not understanding that your role is to motivate is one of the biggest mistakes salon owners make.*

That's really sad. As a professional, your job is to motivate and inspire people to feel good, to dress in a different way, to want to do their hair, to want to look after their skin. If you don't do that for you, how the hell can you motivate them? It goes deeper. Ruby's boss is an immaculately dressed woman. She should have motivated Ruby along the way, helping her understand that her presentation is super important. But equally so, when I've been in there in her salon waiting for my service with the threader, I've seen Ruby covering for her boss because she's late!

Running in to Ruby got me thinking about how critical team motivation is in our industry. How much motivating of your team should you do? I'll measure it for you to make it easier, but I'll bet one thing ... you definitely should be doing more motivating than you are now. Twice as much. An absolute truckload. In fact, a truckload and a trailer, as well. Not understanding that your role is to motivate is one of the biggest mistakes salon owners make.

I motivate you. You motivate your team. Your team motivates your clients. It simply rolls down the hill. You wouldn't expect your clients to come in and motivate your staff, would you? And you certainly wouldn't expect your staff to show up at work to motivate you. That's backwards. You have to keep finding ways to praise people for the little things they do. Don't tell me it's impossible. There's always something to praise or someone to compliment. You can thank someone for always looking their best when they come to work or for always being at work on time and ready for action.

In the past, we've caught people doing things we don't like and we complain. Yet, when we see them doing something good, we often take it for granted. You need to flip that approach on its head and start praising more.

Some of you might be thinking that's what you pay them to do. That's true, you do. But imagine if you applied that same thinking in a marriage or relationship. *Why do I have to say I love her? She knows I love her. I told her already. Why do I have to do keep telling her that's why I married her? Clearly she has a memory problem.*

It's the same thing in the salon – everyone wants (even, needs) to feel valued. Everyone wants to feel important. If that means you telling them the blatantly obvious, then that's what you do. Try it, you'll be surprised.

You're reading this book because you're looking for some tips, some tricks, some answers as to why your team is average, why they're running hot and cold. You can prise them out of the average box and into the OMG-they-are-awesome box by motivating them, then praising them, then praising them again. Keep motivating them by your sheer presence and energy.

Trust me, praising and believing in someone that they can do great things will make an enormous difference to their belief in themselves and, in turn, to their attitude and professional performance in your salon.

Plus two – upping an attitude score by two points.

You know those blow-up clowns that are weighted in the base and no matter how hard you push them away, the little smart arses keep coming right back at you? Your team members with crappy attitudes are just the same. You know … one bad comment away and they come right back at you with another. It doesn't matter how hard you work at pushing away the bad attitude, it just comes right back at you. It's exhausting!

> *You need to help them understand that their job is to keep their share of the morale up.*

First you need to know what I mean by an attitude score. When I start coaching a salon owner, I need to get a sense of the team that I'll be working with. One of the quickest ways is to ask the salon owner to score each team member out of 10 according to their attitude towards the business and life in general.

When you're running a salon you have to make decisions mostly based on facts (not on emotions). Sometimes you have to make those decisions fast. Me asking *How many out of 10?* gives me and the salon owner some facts to work with. I start to hear: *She is definitely an eight or nine. He's a 10. She's about a seven. Mmmm ... a two.*

The good news is that I know I can raise each of those numbers by two points. I don't think I've ever met a team member who I couldn't raise by at least two points. Keeping them there is another story

Often your team members aren't aware how much their attitude impacts the rest of the team. You need to help them understand that their job is to keep their share of the morale up. When you see examples of this happening and you gently point them out, the person gradually gets that it's just not fair to spread the stink and bring the whole team down.

You'll easily spot the low scorers. They always think that what everyone else has agreed on will not work. They constantly point out where the holes are in any of your plans rather than seeing the potential. They're hard work. And they're painful.

Imagine your highest scoring team member for attitude is Suzanne. She's a nine. Now imagine your salon environment if you had six Suzannes. How would that affect your business? It would be awesome, right? Now imagine the blow-up clown type you just scored two out 10 is Julie. How would your salon look if you had six Julies? It's frightening. Yes? You'd feel like shutting the doors and walking away.

I'd say you already know what good attitude is and you know what challenging is. You already found one awesome person, so why do you tolerate less? And, there's the core problem: that you settle for less.

Chasing dollars is up hill.
Servicing clients is down hill.

To create lasting change you (the salon owner) need to be the mentor. My job is to coach you to be the mentor. Your job is to raise the standard across the board and constantly want to take your team to the next level. Maybe your salon is a C-grade, then your challenge is to get them into the B-grade finals. Maybe you spend some months there and then you raise the standard again. Before you know it, you're playing A-grade. It takes time and you need to use every win along the way as an opportunity to praise your team members' contributions.

You also have to look at your own attitude score. I've witnessed incredible change in salon owners who've been in the industry 25 years. They've achieved an increase in their team members of around four points each! I keep reminding them to ask the team after every win, big or small, to reflect on the change they made.

Why did you recommend so much retail?

Why have your retail sales gone up?

Why has your rebooking improved?

Your Salon Team

Why is your appearance better than ever before?

Why are you arriving at work on time, sometimes even early?

Unless you acknowledge each change right there and then when you get the behaviour you want, they won't be aware of it and it won't stick.

What came through time and time again was that the owner had changed her own behaviour and attitude. For the first time ever the team felt like it wasn't about the money, it was about the clients. When team members feel that you make money at the expense of them making an effort, they don't respond well. What they do like is seeing that the clients are getting exceptional service. Money is a by-product of great service. Improve your service and you'll improve your returns.

> **Money is a by-product of great service. Improve your service and you'll improve your returns.**

Think of it like a mountain. If the money is at the summit, your first thought is the money and having to push your way up to the top to reach the dollars. It's going to be hard work – it's all up hill. If you're at the top of the mountain and the money is at the bottom, meaning it's your last thought, then you can just get on with your job of looking after your team, checking in on their attitudes, making sure they have all the tools and equipment they need, making sure they have the direction and guidelines to know how you look after clients in your salon. The energy ball just rolls from one person to the next. Everyone shares the load and the thinking just flows because the one thing you all have in mind is customer service. The ball will roll right down to the bottom where the money is. It's not up hill thinking, it's just a natural thing that happens. People love you, they trust you and they take your recommendations. It's a simple progression, a natural by-product from looking after clients well.

The Nitty Gritty.

A truckload of motivation is still not enough.

Motivating your team is your role.

Praise people for the little things.

Keep praising over and over.

Attitude scores give you and your business coach facts to work with.

You already know what awesome is; don't settle for less.

Be consistent to make the change stick.

Money is a by-product of great service, and great service is all about attitude.

chapter 11

11

The problem: is it you or them? Are you being too flexible?

Way back in my first salon I hired a new junior, let's call her Louise. She'd worked part-time at the chemist just up the street and at the interview Louise seemed lovely and super keen. After a few weeks I noticed little things like that she was always a minute or two late back from lunch and that her mood wasn't always even. Then I got a wake-up call. Literally. The chemist owner phoned to warn me Louise had stolen from his business while working for him and that I should watch her carefully. He had camera footage to prove his claim; it wasn't just gossip. We were part of a country town community and he felt I should know. I never let on to Louise that I knew about her past but I did keep an extremely close eye on her from then on. Her performance kept deteriorating and before long I worked her through a couple of warnings, and then let her go. It wasn't an easy time. And it was a big lesson for me. I created the problem in my salon and I could have saved myself all that angst by simply phoning Louise's previous employer before inviting her to join my team. The chemist's name and phone number were right there on her CV. Never again … I have never employed anyone since without first checking their references.

> *You decide who should and who shouldn't be on your team.*

Remember this tale when you're wondering who causes the problems in your salon. It's like when you're trying to end a relationship and you say, "It's not you, it's me". It's the same in the salon, because you're the decision-maker. You decide who should and who shouldn't be on your team. You call the shots. If there's a problem with your team, it's 100% your fault.

The real question to ask yourself is: *Why do I tolerate people in my team who consistently underperform? People who have a stinky attitude that doesn't fit?* Mostly, it's because nobody taught you how to be honest about it and how to deal with the emotional side of leading your team. You haven't set high enough standards for yourself and you believe that there isn't anyone else out there.

Many salon owners are reluctant to employ new people for fear they'll be stuck with them long after they don't work out. It's a valid fear because almost everyone presents better in an interview than they actually turn out to be a month later. You can hedge your bets, though.

Checking references is fundamental (once you've learnt the lesson). But you can do more to protect yourself. The key is to be honest and have clear checkpoints when you're hiring. You're allowed to say, "I'd like to see more before I commit". It's good business practice to allow a one-day trade test or a day's trial. Then, if you decide to invite them to join your team, you're allowed to make it clear that you'll be reviewing their performance closely. In my book, you're more than allowed, you're obligated. Sit down with them at the end of the first week and have a review. At the end of the first month, have another review. You MUST have a one-on-one meeting each week – it'll give you both an opportunity to discuss any issues and reinforce expectations. And it will give you a chance to work on those problem issues like punctuality and physical appearance that commonly creep into the equation after the hiring's done and can really bring the standard of your team down.

I gave you this position. It's a gift. It's up to you to keep it.

As a leader, you control the culture of your team and your salon. Once you've established a clear, strong culture in your business, you'll find it easier to find new team members who fit. Your business culture determines the standards you and your team uphold. If you tolerate less than you should when it comes to consistency in performance, you will always struggle with mediocrity. It's true: it's really difficult to find good team members. But it's also really difficult to find a great boss. Great bosses understand the culture of their businesses. If you settle for average and turned a blind eye to things you know are not in the best interest of your business, you leave the door wide open for the service level to drop. Any drop in service level will eventually eat into your profits and produce a downturn in business.

Paint a picture of what you want.

You don't need to be harsh or bossy to be a great leader. Being crystal clear on what you want is a big part of effective leadership. Paint the picture of how you expect a person to behave. And if you frame it as "asking for help" rather a demand, you might just get what you wish for.

Recently, a salon owner who I'm mentoring mentioned that he was nervous because his 2IC was going on leave and his other senior always has trouble getting to work on time. Her clients love her, her skill set is great, but she's a touch airy-fairy and unfocussed. Yet, her lack of punctuality is the first thing her boss brings up when he's worrying about someone else going on leave. He doesn't want clients waiting outside the salon for his team to arrive.

He said, "I'm going to tell her that she has to be there at 8.30. She just has to."

I said "Instead, why don't you tell her you're in a bit of a spot and ask if she can help you? Now, this kid is a good kid, she really is. I know that if you ask her to help you, she will. Instead of telling her, I need you ask her. *Can you help me out by being at work half an hour earlier just those two days while the 2IC is away? I'd really appreciate you doing this for me.*"

> *Paint the picture of how you expect a person to behave.*

It's interesting that there are so many different ways to try and get a result. My suggestion offered an engagement opportunity, to help the team member feel good about her part rather than cornered or pressured. That's what I mean by framing your request. Most people, when you ask them nicely and explain the reason, are more than willing to help.

Think of this every time you need to paint the picture of where you're taking your business. Break up the tasks you want to get done and ask your team, "Who would like to help me do some of these tasks?" Maybe it's writing a job ad to go on the salon window, posting on your social media or ordering stock. Try saying, "These are the tasks I need to get done this week. If anyone could help me out with them, I'd be grateful."

The right people for you are the ones who are like-minded, who enjoy being in a team, who don't think the world owes them a living, who are eager to lend a hand and share their knowledge.

Find these people, because they're out there looking for you. And please, please stop settling for less because that's what's holding you back and it's going to lead to disappointment, over and over again. Raise the bar when it comes to your energy and effort toward yourself and your business and you'll be surprised what happens next.

If you think you can, you can and if you think you can't, you can't. It starts in your head. It's you, not them.

How much is too much flexibility?

When my daughter Tess was about seven, my mother came to stay with us. Because my daughter had a queen-size bed, I put them in together. Tess was always excited about sharing a bed with Grandma. In the morning Tess came out to the kitchen and told me she'd only made half the bed because Grandma was still in the other half. I went up to see how that looked and Tess was right: there was Grandma all tucked in like you might find a wrap in the sandwich shop.

Your Salon Team

It made me smile and we still all laugh about it today. Tess was being flexible. She knew she was expected to make her bed each morning and she showed initiative and flexibility in finding a way around the problem. As an adult, Tess still never thinks she can't do something; she always thinks about how she can do it. I wonder where she gets that from?

In the salon, where do you draw the line between being flexible enough to leave room for your team to use their initiative and keeping control of your business culture?

For me, there are not too many things I'm happy to be flexible about because I'm really clear on what I want to get done. In my early days as a salon owner, I was more flexible because I was trying to please everyone. Now I know it's impossible to please everyone and I suspect most of you will agree on that.

When you have a common thread that stitches you all together, you don't have to be flexible. In my business the common thread is the client experience – and I won't let anything compromise it. So, I've always been flexible on things like my team's sense of style, on tattoos and piercings. I do think you need to fit into your environment. It's a bit like vegans – you don't see them working in a butcher shop. People want to work where they fit in and feel valued.

I'm flexible on how quickly people learn and on things like where the team want to have their Christmas party. I was always flexible on how my salon team went about doing tasks for me, like the till. They could please themselves whether they added up the EFTPOS dockets first or counted the cash first, as long as they ticked all the boxes and I had everything I needed in the safe. In most cases, so long as the task is done, I'm happy.

I've always worked hard at cultivating initiative, in my children – my Team Family – as well as in my salon team. Having people in your team who take initiative and step-up without having to run to you for permission is a great place to be. I like people who don't stop at the first sign of something in their way or when things seem a little different.

Everyone adds value to your team in some way so if your junior wants to rewrite the list of chores her way, let her. In fact, encourage it. The more your team take ownership of their roles, the better it is for you and your business.

> **Make your salon the best place your team members have ever worked.**

Take rebooking salon clients, for example. Some team members like to mention the rebooking during the service, perhaps when the colour is processing. That's when they choose to have a chat around when they think is best to see their client next. Other people on your team might prefer to do it near the end of the service, perhaps when the blow wave is coming together and the client is actually watching the results unfold and is excited about the transformation. Either way, I don't mind as long as your rebooking percentage is above 75%. What I don't want to hear is a client being asked at the last minute, as they're about to leave the salon, "Do you want to rebook?" It's lazy and I guarantee the team member who asks this way has a rebooking rate way below 75%. It's like chalk on a blackboard to me – I can't stand that type of near-enough-is-good-enough attitude. It directly affects my clients' service so I'm not flexible. I'm also inflexible on mood swings, energy levels, punctuality and presentation, because they all affect my clients' experience and that affects the stability of my business, which in turn makes my job unstable.

I've learnt over the years that "give and take" does not work with all team members. With give and take, you have to constantly keep score. People seem to remember things in their favour before they remember them in your favour. They remember that they stayed back 15 minutes late to finish a client but they don't recall why (they were talking too much and that's why they ran over by 15 minutes). They also forget that sometimes, even though their lunch break was cut short, you allowed them to duck off to the post office to pay their phone bill before it got cut off.

Some team members ask if they can miss their lunch and leave an hour early today. My answer is, "No. Missing your lunch is perhaps one of the silliest ideas ever. People should get lunch breaks; food is fuel so why would you run low on fuel. It's not in the best interest of your clients for you to work straight through without a break. Gone are the days when hairdressers were living on cigarettes and coffee. If we can work something out, you can leave an hour early today, but you can't miss your lunch. You'll need to make up that hour later on this week."

It's just too hard to keep score. As the leader of the team, you've got far bigger things you need to be working on, and the biggest one of all is to make your salon the best place your team members have ever worked.

Your number one job is to fill your salon with amazing clients who absolutely treasure their experience here and to train, nurture and develop the most passionate team of professionals you've ever worked with. Growing your salon business through marketing is something you take very seriously. You don't want to be bogged down by keeping score of trivial things such as someone who left 15 minutes early to get to a yoga class. Ask them to find another yoga class they can comfortably get to. Work hours are work hours. Your team members should be getting on with the task of creating an exceptional experience for every client, especially the last one of the day. When they're watching the clock ready to escape, they're not giving clients their full attention.

What we all want is every column of every day filled with quality clients. It doesn't happen by accident, it happens by intention. Never be flexible on the quality of service you and your team deliver.

The Nitty Gritty.

You call the shots. Period.

Have honest, clear checkpoints when you're hiring.

A solid salon culture makes it easier to hire and motivate the right people.

Be clear on what you want; paint a picture.

Ask, rather than demand.

Leave enough room for initiative.

Never compromise on things that affect customer experience.

Give and take doesn't work – it might in the short-term, but it won't in the long-term.

Work on the big stuff, like filling your salon with amazing clients.

chapter 12

12

12

Targets: why, what, when and how?

Have you ever seen the joy in a team member's face when they hit their target? I have. Many times. And it's still magical, every single time. Whether it's a team target or an individual target, it's cause for celebration and a positive signpost on your salon's journey from good to great.

Salon targets come in many forms. Some are based on money and others on number of services or products sold. I believe you need them all to run a booming salon business. Targets seem to be tricky to get your head around. So grab a cuppa and settle in for a lengthy chapter as I tell you what I've learned about them over many years in the industry.

In almost all other industries, it's normal to have targets that must be met. Most people in hair and beauty have a strong opinion on whether targets work in general, and on whether team targets work better than individual ones. Some people feel that targets push their team into the uncomfortable zone where if you don't win, you lose. That's rubbish! High achievers

12

earn that label because they put in the hard work. They're the ones you want to be sharing your profit with. Like everything in life, it's all in the way you present the package.

As a business coach, I've opted out of working with some salon owners simply because they didn't want to implement targets at all, they didn't want their team members to know what kind of money they make for the business. I don't get that sort of thinking. If someone's a great earner for your business, why not reward them? In fact, if you don't, they will certainly move on, and I wouldn't blame them.

Show me the money (because I love money).

Money is not a bad thing. It gives you choices. It provides peace of mind and security. When I think back to when I've been most stressed, it was always about my financial situation. As an industry, we need to get over the discomfort we have around money targets and understand that, in business, money is a measure. If your team members aren't doing a minimum of 3.5 times their gross wage, that's a business problem you need to address. You can change things by understanding your true value. Part of that is having a goal and aiming at a target or some line in the sand that says this is a minimum requirement. The trouble I see around targets is that many salon owners don't nurture and encourage their team members to grow in skill and confidence so that consistently reaching a target is a real option. Often a target is thrown at somebody without breaking it down and explaining to the person how it might be achieved. Targets are not a set-and-forget option and there is a correct time and place as to when to introduce them.

Not all targets are created equal.

Every single person in your business needs to have an individual target. Your junior might need be able to deliver a shampoo and conditioner on a client in five minutes. Or you might ask her to find three models every week for a tint application. Or someone else to recommend and deliver five basin services a week. If your target is money-based, you need to explain what it is your team member needs to learn in order to hit your target. Break it into bite-size bits for them.

In beauty, a target might be to deliver a number of microdermabrasions or lash extensions in a week. In hair, it might be to deliver basin services. Individual targets mean that you reward the individual, and group targets mean that you reward the group. You need to try both to see how your team responds. I favour setting challenges around services rather

> *If your team aren't doing a minimum of 3.5 times their gross wage, that's a business problem you need to address.*

than the money. All targets or goals have to use numbers but, for some reason, team members don't enjoy celebrating wins that are purely money related. Service-based targets are about the overall care of your clients. If you continue to raise the level of service, more money will naturally come your way.

Try this one tomorrow.

This is a simple, do-able team challenge. Set the target that every client, for the entire day, leaves your salon with a sample. It might be of a hero product like sunscreen. There's not one person on this planet who wouldn't be interested in a sunscreen sample. And most people would be open to knowing more about sunscreen – there are so many types available at so many price points. They come in roll-ons, sprays, creams, oils, mousses and tinted moisturisers. It's overwhelming, so why not include an FAQs sheet with the sample? I bet you'll find your sunscreen sales booming. Imagine what might happen if you extended the target to a week or a month. Why not do it and find out?

Or this one.

In hair, your hero product might be a heat protector. Let me share a little insider trick with you. Get your client to put both hands out in front of you. Apply the heat protector to the back of one hand (if it's a spray, avoid overspray on the other hand). Give it a few minutes to dry then grab your hairdryer and blow the hot air across both hands. Your client will find themselves pulling back the untreated hand while the other is protected from the heat by the product. They'll be blown away (excuse the pun) by how effective it is. Now use the heat protector on their hair today. If they don't want to take it today, offer a take-home sample. It's sharing of knowledge like this that will take your team members' average thinking (*my clients have everything*) to actually being proactive and taking those product sales to a whole new level. Why not try setting a target around that little insider trick and see what happens?

More target talk.

Targets have long had a bad wrap in the hair and beauty industry because most salon owners don't deliver the idea or concept of a target; they focus on a money target and fail to understand that there are many types of targets.

Targets are often dropped on team members without explanation – why it's important, how to go about it or what the reward is when it's reached.

I always prefer to introduce targets only when the team is already in reach of hitting the target, so they can actually see that with a little bit more focus, it's do-able. Setting unrealistic targets benefits no one.

To me, targets are a way of showcasing people who do well. Other than core targets (more about that later) you should change targets often to keep interest up. Use different products or services to focus on. Get your product rep's on board and get creative.

Always put a timeframe on any target. Everything needs to be on a suck-it-and-see basis. Revisit the target after a week, a month or three months so you're not locked into something you wish you hadn't started. Often, I find myself helping salon owners remove existing targets because they don't work, are not fair to everyone or are either way too low (that you are sharing profit that you don't have) or too high (that the team member doesn't even try).

> *Cash payments, like mullets, are long gone!*

I worked with one salon where the team members added up their own targets over the course of the week and when the Saturday was finished, would help themselves to a cash bonus straight from the till on their way out the door. "Took my $50. See ya!" OMG!

The nuts and bolts of core targets (aka profit share).

We have a lot to think about when it comes to paying target bonuses. Your team members get regular, consistent pay that comes with sick leave and holiday pay. If you want to go over and beyond that, then you're really talking about profit share and there has to be a profit to share.

I believe profit share is better delivered over three weeks and definitely not over a single week. It should only be given to a team member who consistently brings in more than 3.5 times their gross wage. In beauty, it can be more like 4 to 5 times as very high machinery costs need to be factored in. "Consistently" cannot be measured over a single week. This longer timeframe also gives your team members time to make up for events like public holidays or sick days.

Here's an example. Let's say that Mandy's target is $4,000 in any single week or $12,000 over three weeks.

In the first week Mandy might do:	$4037
In the second week:	$3850
And in the last week:	$4542

Even though in the second week, she was $150 short of target, overall her total is $12,429, which comes in over the $12,000. This means Mandy gets her bonus for that three-week period. Not forgetting that she already has a base rate of pay including annual leave public holiday pay and sick pay.

Her "profit share" might be 5% of the whole, which is $621.45 on top of her existing base pay. This amount needs to be taxed, the same as all money paid to an employee.

Many team members feel the tax is a mean trick. In fact, it's the law. Cash payments, like mullets, are long gone!

12

Retail targets are part of the deal.

Retails sales are not a separate thing to service sales. Servicing a client is done as a whole, so the profit share (or money) target should include both. This approach gives your team a different mindset around retail, not as something you add-on sell or treat separately. Looking after any clients in any salon in any country in the world should have a holistic approach. Here's a sample of how you should think:

What are my client's problems/challenges?

How can I make suggestions around the solutions?

How can I change what I have here in front of me?

How is my client going to look after themselves when I'm not there?

What lessons do I need to teach?

What tips and tricks do I need to share?

What products do my client need to take home with them to reproduce what I did here today?

Nail that, make that the focus every day with every client and I guarantee you'll soon be looking at ways you can share your profit with your team members.

You've got to walk before you can run.

If your team is telling you they need to be paid more, that they are incredibly valuable to you, then take a look at the loyalty of their client base. They need to be above 75% rebooking. Retail sales need to consistently sit at 20% of their overall takings or minimum of 15 units per week or three units a day. In beauty, you could double that and have your retail sales sit at 40%. Of course, every salon is different – these figures are a guide to get you thinking.

I don't know of any salon owner who wasn't prepared to share the profit with their team members. But I do know of many who simply don't have consistent profit to share. So perhaps the answer is to make your targets around service-based challenges until you raise the standard across the board and are ready to enter into money-based targets.

Let your team know where you're heading, why you're doing it in this particular order and ask them to support you along the way. Invite them along for the ride!

12

The Nitty Gritty.

Targets are tricky, but well worth the effort of working out the one that's right for your team.

They're not a set-and-forget option.

Explain each target to your team.

Always set timeframes for targets.

Try individual and team targets.

Profit share is not a dirty word (or two).

Total retail sales and service sales together.

chapter 13

13

What meerkats and Indian givers can teach you about sharing the load and motivating your team.

What do meerkats and Indian givers have to do with training your team? Let's start with the meerkat and how to recognise it in the wild (and your salon). A client who's usually in your column phones your salon, needing a blow-wave at short notice. You suggest someone else on your team will look after her.

She comes in and your team member gets on with the job of looking after her. Then you notice that instead of the usual blow-wave, your client seems to be getting a haircut, even though you thought she wanted to grow her hair. So, like a meerkat, you're stretching your neck, trying to see what's going on. Like a hawk, you excuse yourself from your client and you're over there in a flash. You do your best to disguise the stickybeak in you. But now the stylist has to explain to you, in front of the client, why they've chosen to do a haircut.

Really? You have to check up? Why can't you trust that your team member knows what she's doing? And that your client also knows what she's doing? I call it being a meerkat. You've instilled into the client that you have to watch your staff, that they can't make decisions on their own. And, you've instilled in the stylist that you don't trust them, that they can't do a proper consultation without your approval.

> **Why can't you trust that your team member knows what she's doing?**

I know. It's not your intention. But, like it or not, that's how it comes across. You wonder why people on your team don't grow past you — it's because your meerkat behaviour undermines and holds them back. You're frightened that if you don't keep an eye on them, they'll get it wrong and you'll lose the client. I get where you coming from. I really do. This client just needs to know that you'll be there if needed and when invited to be.

There's a real difference – the invited bit.

You can see meerkats in the wild in the grasslands of Africa. That's their natural habitat. You can also see them in zoos and salons all over the world. Spot them easily (in either zoo or salon) by their out-stretched necks as they try to suss out what's going on somewhere that's not where they actually are. They're curious little critters, and interfering by nature, always sticking their nose into other people's business. I'm not so sure why they do it in the wild or in the zoo. Probably it's a survival mechanism. The reason they do it in the salon is that they feel their heads are on the chopping block if things don't go to plan. Sure, if your client isn't happy and doesn't return, it's an expensive mistake. The trouble with adopting meerkat behaviour is that you're showing your team member you don't trust are showing the person you're working with that you don't trust them. No one likes being watched over and second-guessed. Not even you. And no one learns much when they feel scrutinised.

You need to get your act together when it comes to your training. Because if your training plan is effective and the results reflect an eight or a nine out of ten, then you'll be more confident letting your team member work on a client without you stretching and neck meerkat-style to keep an eye on them. And they'll be more confident about using their initiative. True? It's not only exhausting being a meerkat, it holds you back from having a team who can think for themselves and act accordingly.

13

What about the Indian giver?

Wanting your team to step up and letting them step up are two different things. Once again, being an Indian giver to your team, means you're sending them mixed messages.

I notice many salon owners wanting their team members to step-up and take responsibility for things. At least, that's what they tell me they want. The reality is quite different. In practice, they're holding their team back with their Indian giver behaviour.

When I was a kid, we called some people Indian givers. I have no idea where the term comes from and it quite possibly isn't politically correct these days. But, bear with me, anyway. As kids we used the term Indian giver to describe someone who gave you something, then changed their mind and took it back. For example, perhaps my sister said "You can have my blue jumper. I don't wear it anymore." Thank you! Then when she saw it on me, it looked so good (I had a decent set of boobs; she didn't) she decided she wanted it back and that she shouldn't have given to me in the first place.

Why am I telling you this? In salons, many of you are doing similar things with your team members. You start by saying I'd like you to do *blah, blah, blah*. But, for some reason or another you don't let them do what you asked and it's often halfway through the delivery that you change your mind. Your team member never learns what it feels like to take responsibility for the whole task. And, if it doesn't go exactly to plan, you – the fixer – swoop in and take it back off them completely. Sound like anyone you know?

Imagine I'm standing in front of you and I ask if you could call Mark the product rep. I hand you a piece of paper with a list of the products I want to order, a couple of testers and a note about a product that arrived broken in the last order. I tell you the list needs to be either scanned or read out over the phone to Mark. Then I look at the list and decide it's too difficult for you and, before I've given you a chance, I take it back and make the call myself. There, right there – I'm an Indian giver.

If you want someone to do something for you – and you should – then you need to take the time to brief them properly. Ask them if they have any questions and whether or not they understand what you need them to do. To check this, get them to explain it back to you. Once you believe they've got it right, let them get on with it so they can really learn what it's like to be in your shoes.

The key is to take the time in the beginning. Pre-frame what might happen and what might not happen and what to do about it, if it does or doesn't. When you bother to explain things to people properly, they have a better understanding and also a far greater chance of success. And that's good for you both, right?

Let's face it what's the worst that can happen? They get it wrong and then you get them to fix it. Remember, people learn from experiences. There are no mistakes in life just lessons.

13

Learn to share the load.

I got married and a week later so did some friends of my husband. Both Rita and I were hairdressers. By luck, we ended up on the Greek Islands for our honeymoon at the exact same time. We had our first babies a few months apart and our second babies a day apart (only that time I had twins). We even ended up in the same maternity hospital. It was spooky how often our lives ran parallel.

I remember going to see her when our first babies were about three years old. She had her little man sitting on the kitchen bench, spoon-feeding him. I could see she had a high chair and I said, "Why don't you let him do it himself?"

"It's too slow," she said. "And he makes too much mess. This is way faster."

I thought, *How is he ever going to learn?*

It didn't matter to her that he was being spoon-fed. I'm fairly sure she isn't still doing it because both our first-borns, Michael and Tess, are now 26-year-old doctors. They must have worked it out despite their parents having completely different approaches to parenting. My point is that you don't have to make it so hard for yourself like Rita did with the spoon-feeding. I'm sure Rita thought it wasn't hard and that I was cleaning up unnecessary mess. Rita was a stay-at-home mum and I worked part-time right through having my kids. I let my kids feed themselves as I got on with other things. Sometimes I'd return to a mammoth mess. I remember once taking the high chair outside and washing it down with the garden hose. I liked strapping them into the high chair. They were safe, even though the cat walking past wasn't. Once I came back to the room to Tess saying "gone" and the cat busily licking a Weetabix off her back. Tess saying "gone" was referring to her breakfast. That wouldn't have happened at Rita's house.

Always taking the quicker route can be a double-edged sword. There's an old saying that goes like this: *If you want something done, ask a busy person.* For them, it's not much trouble, they just find a way to get it done. Although that's all absolutely true, sometimes people ride on the fact that you're impatient and would rather do it yourself than wait for anyone else to do it.

The trouble with that thinking is that if you're ever away on leave or sick, no one knows what you do because you've never shared it. That's a really unhealthy way to run a business. I call it small thinking and it's one of the things that hobbles great salon technicians and stops them become great salon owners. They either don't know how to or refuse to let anyone help share their load. They keep doing everything themselves, because it seems quicker. The truth is if you give the people around you an opportunity to learn and practise, there's every chance they'll soon be doing the tasks just as quickly as you. Maybe even quicker.

If you know your time would be better used somewhere else, then hand over the jobs you feel have the lowest value. Do what you feel is what will help you reach your goals the most. Just think about it long-term, not only short-term.

13

I've never tried, nor will I ever try, to do my own bookwork. YUK! I wouldn't enjoy it and would have to pay someone twice as much to fix it up. So, do what you love and hand over the rest to your team. They want to part to be a part of the business and the salon's future. Rita didn't mind feeding Michael until he was three. I did, because it didn't fit into my plan. It wasn't helpful to me reaching my long-term goals.

There's only one thing in your business that you can't get anyone else to do. I bet you can't guess what it is. Everything that you do, someone else can do it for you – from paying the accounts to ordering stock and training people. The only thing they can't do is sign your name. That's it really.

Businesses are either going forwards or backwards. They don't stay the same. As people, we should take on that same thinking. Your business will not remain the same, even if you want it to. Your team will be going backwards of forwards. You will be going backwards or forwards. There are all sorts of ways to keep your business, your team and yourself moving in the right direction. One of the keys is learning to hand over to those around you, to your team, to your suppliers, to your experts like your bookkeeper. Share the load and free yourself up for what you love.

The Nitty Gritty.

Don't watch over your team members like a meerkat.

Show them you trust them to get on with it and let you know when there's an issue.

Indian giver behaviour prevents your team members from learning.

Let them make mistakes. Let them fix it. Let them learn.

Doing it yourself is not always the quickest way.

Consider the long-term outcomes.

Share the load and let your team step-up to help.

chapter 14

14

Creating a negative-free salon zone – we all just want to have fun.

I once worked in a salon with a team of mostly pleasant people. Sarah was not so pleasant. She always managed to find the dark side of any person or situation. Hers were the worst clients ever. Sarah never had a simple cold – it was always full-blown 'flu. Her landlord was an ogre. Her dog even pissed her off. You know the sort: she was never happy unless she was having a bitch about someone or something. It was easy to fall into the trap of joining her on the dark side, dropping your guard and having a full-on bitch session with her in the backroom. One-by-one the staff around me joined Sarah on "Team Negative" – I resisted; I always err on the perky side rather than glass-half-empty. In the end, I found myself fighting for my right NOT to bitch. I felt like an outsider because I had a positive attitude. I resolved, then and there, that when I owned a salon, I would make sure it was a negative-free zone.

I know: some people thrive on a big-arse dose of drama. So why would you want to have a salon free from drama and negativity? Try these for starters:

- You want your salon to be recognised as a workplace of choice, so you can attract the best people to your team.
- Bullying thrives in a negative or toxic environment; as boss, you have an obligation to prevent bullying.
- Negativity attracts negativity (see my tale above).

My own salon's culture was "love it" and set the tone for an environment where clients and staff alike had no tolerance for that long-faced downer person. We agreed we didn't need any negative shit where we worked and spent so much time together.

We had a way of bringing a sense of humour to anyone with a long face. These faces are easy to spot among the females on your team: they're without proper makeup application and never any lipstick. I always told the girls I'd rather they wore and no undies. Nobody knows about your undies but lipstick is right there for everyone to see. True?

It's as though they think you should be pleased they showed up to work at all. I always say: "When you walk in that door you have chosen. No matter what shit is going down in your private world, you have made a decision that you can work. That's why you walked through that door, so you do everything at 100%. If you can't work, for whatever reason, then you must choose not to walk through that door. It's your decision not mine. If you decide you can't be at work that day, then you must follow the appropriate channels on calling in absent."

It's not for the salon owner to decide whether a reason for being sad, negative or generally displaced is genuine enough to justify a sad face, all that negative energy or a not-coming-in-today phone call. Don't ask questions to determine whether or not your team member's reasoning is good enough – that's just adding to the drama. Better to give them some home truths: "Whatever the reason behind your long face, I can tell you it will still be there when you get home. Why don't you treat your workplace as an oasis that is both drama and negative free? Think of work more like somewhere you can escape what awaits you when you end your shift. At work we simply don't have the luxury of staying in a stinky mood. Your clients are expecting a high standard of service from you. Your teammates are relying on you, so I suggest you consider them first. You'll be surprised that if you decide to lift your game, you can."

I used to have fun with my girls and if I spotted a long face without lipstick, I'd say: "Do you want a hug because I've got a spare one or would you like to use the magic SS super door?" I'd then take them to the salon's front door and point to the top, saying, "It cost me a lot of money to have this door installed but it's so worth it because it's incredibly smart.

14

If you come through this door with an attitude score of anything less than a nine, it will shave off the shitty attitude. That's why it's called a shit shaver. Perhaps it wasn't working right this morning. I think you need to back it up and go through a couple of times more to lift your attitude back up to nine out of ten so you can deliver the customer experience our clients expect from us."

> *A crack is much easier to fix than a big gaping hole.*

It worked every time and it can work in your salon, too. As long as you're not a smart-arse about it and explain why it's important for everyone to bring their A game.

I've always believed that in a salon you should be able to have your lunch break free of any client talk, good or bad. One day in a team meeting I asked the girls if they were interested in helping me make it a negative-free zone. They all supported me 100%.

Unlike many salons, I had a 30-minute team meeting each Friday morning and every team member also had a 20-minute one-to-one meeting with me each week. There was plenty of time to have a whinge about things that perhaps didn't go to plan. I couldn't see why anyone needed to be anything else but positive in my workspace.

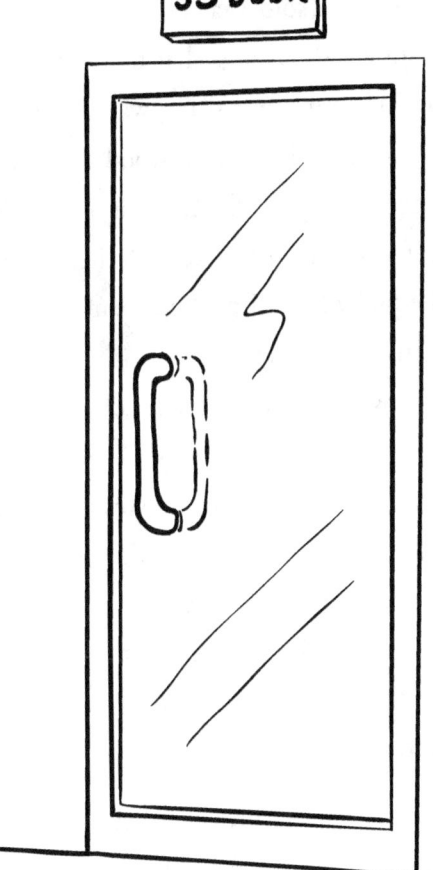

14

If things were not right, then of course I wanted to know about it. But I had no interest in negative conversation just for the sake of it. If I wanted to say something negative about anyone, all we had to do was step outside the salon onto the footpath, say what was needed and then step back in through that magic door. When I sold that business, I got my team members to write down the things that that they liked about working with me. The stand-out thing was that I didn't take any bullshit. They knew where they stood and that if they were being a dickhead, I'd call them on it. They all felt my salon environment was fair and that, although I was a hard marker, I praised equally hard. I pushed them to be their best and taught them that being critiqued was a normal way to find out where to grow. For a very, very small space where nine women worked, it was a bitch-free zone. They all knew what was expected of them, what I would and wouldn't tolerate, and they never had to guess what I was thinking. I told them there and then. People who say, "I didn't get time to say something to a team member" are fooling themselves. You simply make the time. It talks less than a minute to say, "excuse me, lift your game". And they will.

I know it's easy to be misinterpreted or misunderstood in a workplace. You need to jump on any work-related situation when a small crack appears, before the whole thing breaks open. You need to have honest conversations to find out what's really going on. It's a good rule to never let the sun go down on a negative situation, even if it means you have to talk it out on the phone on the way home in the car. You might well end up in an emergency coffee meeting the next morning before the salon opens. But that's the sort of things good salon owners do to lead great teams. A crack is much easier to fix than a a big gaping hole.

Often at the end of a day after my team had all packed up ready to go home, I'd ask one or two people to stay for a five-minute chat. Sometimes it was to thank them. But sometimes I'd delve a little deeper into an issue because I was fierce about making my salon a space where everyone was valued, no one was bullied and we all benefited from it being a truly negative-free zone.

We all just want to have fun.

Jay, one of our ZING coaches, tells me that when he owned a salon he'd often have "a dog and pizza night" in the salon. Don't worry, the dogs didn't eat the pizza. He'd invite the team to all go home after work, collect their dogs and come back. He'd close up the salon, order pizzas, then let the dogs run wild around the salon. They'd eat pizza together and talk all things doggy as they watched the personalities of their pooches unwind. Imagine how much fun that would be if you loved dogs and if everyone on the team actually had or borrowed a dog!

If your salon is all work and no play, it just isn't that much fun. It's dull, boring and no place for you and me. You need to understand you're dealing with people who want to have fun.

14

Our industry is full of creative types who love to have a change of pace, to anticipate, to dial up the tempo now and again. Of course, there's a time and a place for everything. And Jay's fun event wouldn't be so much fun if someone on your team was afraid of dogs … or if your group included cat people.

My point is that you need to plan for some fun in your salon. Let the ideas and the specifics come from your team and you can't go far wrong.

If you plan to have fun and let off some steam together, then it's okay to get on with the job day-to-day. It's like an extra reward or bonus, and recognition that we're all human and enjoy a laugh. It doesn't have to cost the earth and there are endless ideas so you can mix it up and keep your team guessing.

Try this one: choose a busy day of the week and put 15 chocolate bars in a bowl. Announce to your team that it's "chocolate day". Tell them, that every time someone sells a product today, they get to choose a chocolate bar. It's not a challenge as such, but it adds an element of fun to the day.

I remember doing a wine cooler (equal to a Barcardi Breezer for you young things) week along similar lines. Sell a product, you got a wine cooler, meaning in that week if you sold 15 products you got 15 coolers – something the then 18 and 19-year-olds thought was pretty cool. The coolers (or similar) cost about three dollars each if you buy them from one of those big liquor stores.

> **If your salon is *all work* and *no play*, it just isn't that much fun. It's *dull, boring* and *no place for you and me.***

Or you could play *pass the envelope*. Every time someone makes a product sale or offers a service you're particularly promoting, they get handed the envelope. Inside, is a mystery prize, so no one knows what is being handed around. It might be a voucher for a local café, restaurant or petrol station valued at $30-$50.

Every time a retail unit (or the service you nominate) is sold, the envelope moves from one person to the next. As each team member successfully recommends a product or service, they write their name on the envelope and scrub off the previous person's name. This goes on all day until the alarm goes off. You set the alarm at some random time like 3.33 PM and whoever's name is on the envelope when the alarm rings gets the prize. You might set it to go off twice for the day, once close to lunchtime and another nearer closing time. It creates an amazing amount of fun if everyone just relaxes and accepts it for what it is: fun.

You could try a dress-up day where everyone wears a blue wig sourced from those cheap junky stores.

I've known salons to wear their pyjamas and have a pyjama party day.

Others dress up for St Patrick's Day, when everything is green or Valentine's Day, when everything is red.

Your options for injecting fun into your salon are limited only by the imagination of you and your team. Make a resolution to make more fun, more possible, more often and you'll find a tangible lift in the morale of your team.

We all just want to have fun – girls, boys, salon owners and even your clients.

The Nitty Gritty.

As salon owner, you're obliged to provide a safe, healthy workplace.

You must decide every day whether you bring your negativity to work.

Don't tolerate long faces.

Install a magic SS door at your salon.

Ask your team for their support in creating a negative-free zone.

Never let the sun go down on a negative situation.

Without fun, your salon is a dull workplace.

Inject fun to up morale.

There are lots of simple, inexpensive ideas for fun activities.

chapter 15

15

Prepare to parent (because you will).

15

My first boss Sam was a great boss. I worked with him for 16 years. One of the things I most loved about Sam was that he had an Italian upbringing, so he was all about real estate, how to gather houses and how to save money. I'd grown up in a family of nine children where I doubt my parents had given much thought to my financial future. They figured, that as a girl in a Catholic family, it was important for me to be a nice person who someone would want to marry.

But Sam thought differently. He said to me, "You don't know how much you get paid in commissions, do you?" And I didn't. I just opened that pay packet and started pulling out $20 notes to pay for the things I needed. I had no idea how much I was paid. I didn't care; I didn't work for the money, I worked because I loved what I did. Sam said to me, "Why don't I teach you how to save? I'll need one of your bank books, then every week I'll deposit some of your pay." We decided I needed about $380 each week for my expenses. When I hit my target each week, Sam syphoned off $100–$150 and put it away for me. I didn't miss it. One day he said, "Do you know how much money you've got in your bank account?" I had just shy of $1,000 and I had no idea. It was a lot of money in those days and the exercise had taught me that I could save money and plan for my future.

As my boss, Sam had taken on something of a parenting role, educating me about the importance of money. It's hard to believe how different I am today – maybe that's because I came from a place of "no idea" about money.

Like it or not, as a salon owner, you are going to do some parenting. Just like Sam did for me. It might include something as simple as teaching a team member how to budget for their living expenses. I'm surprised how few young people today have any long-term plans, for either their career or financial future. Helping someone budget for the future is a good thing. Some parenting is good – it can be a delight to help someone on your team find their feet and get sorted into a better place.

For some reason, a lot of us get drawn into helping someone who's had a terrible home life. If you're not careful, you can find yourself doing a lot of parenting, the kind of parenting that comes from a disconnected or dysfunctional place. This type of parenting role can be exhausting. It wears on the patience of other team members as well as you, the salon owner. Don't allow all your energy to flow to someone who at their very best is an average team member. Once you get involved, it's hard to let go. The trick is to be careful about who and how you choose to parent, and to stand your ground at the first sign of trouble. I don't know how many times I've heard of a team member doing a sleepover-at-the-boss's-house scenario. *Yuk!* Don't do this.

It's easy to think of parenting as simply discipline – that you'll be disciplining this person to get to work on time, to have pride in their appearance, to be getting into bed at a reasonable hour, to be eating healthy. I'm a parent and I don't do that kind of parenting with my children who are in their early 20s. That sort of self-respect should have long been sorted, probably 10 to 15 years earlier.

If you seem to be spending most of the conversation getting people up to just an average standard, something's not right. Instead, think of your salon-owner-come-parent role as an adviser or educator. Maybe that includes advice about big picture thinking. *Where do you see yourself in three years? What are you saving for?* Perhaps getting them to stick up for themselves if one of their friends is leaning on them a bit heavy. That's all fine, but if you start lending them money or they need to be sleeping on your couch, that's not a healthy or clever choice.

When I looked to find good people to join my team, I was always curious to find out more about their family background and what kind of care factor they placed on relationships. I didn't care if they were raised by their grandmother or in a foster home; family comes in many shapes and sizes today and I am happy with all of them. Family is who you can rely on. What I did care about is how they spoke about whoever family is to them. Ideally, they spoke from the heart and had formed good relationships with loved ones. If I heard hints such as *I don't speak to my dad. My mum is always nagging me. My sister and I don't get on.* – I'd tune into a string of disconnection and a sense that they always had something to complain about or someone to blame.

If, on the other hand, they had an acceptance of the way things were in their world, that they were excited about the future, looking forward and having the support of someone such as a parent, guardian, friend or boyfriend, then I was more comfortable about seriously looking at them as a prospective team member. Even now, I still seek out people who look for the good in any situation. We work in an environment where the hair colour I see as red, someone else might see as honey blonde and someone else might see as gold. Our ability to see and respect the viewpoint of others is super important.

If the person sitting in front of me at an interview can't seem to express themselves in a way that demonstrates they value relationships in their life, then I'm going to be concerned that the common denominator is this person.

Remember: everyone is on his or her best behaviour in an interview. I've found going with my gut instinct never lets me down. If you listen to your instincts, you'll know when a person feels right.

The Nitty Gritty.

You will do some level of parenting of your team.

Do the right kind of parenting - advising and educating.

When hiring, seek out people who value relationships.

chapter 16

16

Your salon's culture – setting clear expectations and tackling tough topics.

16

If I had one wish for every salon owner I've ever worked with, I'd grant them the understanding that business success begins and ends with their salon's culture. It's the start point and the end point – it's like a playbook you can refer to every day, without having to repeat yourself over and over again. Get your salon's culture right and so many other aspects of leading your team will fall magically into place.

I feel so strongly that many problems salon owners have spring from not being clear about who is to do what and when. Your business relies heavily on you as the salon owner. If you don't create and set a strong culture for your salon, then you'll need to be there on deck everyday or when you're not, you'll be on the end of a phone answering silly questions all day. Questions that your team should be able to answer for themselves. What sort of lifestyle is that for you? Where's the freedom and the rewards of being a salon owner if you can't step back and trust your team to carry on without you?

Rather than having a complicated salon manual that gathers dust on a shelf in your backroom, I suggest you develop a succinct list of "rules" that define your salon's culture. Ingrain these rules into your team. Refer to them often and use them as guiding principles, so your members build confidence in making decisions for themselves.

You'll want to create your own list specific to your salon and your team. Here are the ones that have stuck strongest with me throughout my years in the industry. Use these as a starting point.

We fix things once, so that we don't spend our life wasting time fixing it over and over.

Everybody takes initiative and does what they think is right at the time.

We're all different, and we are a team. We celebrate our differences.

Nobody drowns alone because there is always someone to help you. You just have to ask for help – we can't read minds.

The clients belong to the salon. You came without clients. You leave without clients.

Nobody knows everything so don't start sentences with: "I know."

We consider "can't" to be a swearword. It means you have already decided. What we're looking for is: "I'm having difficulty, can you help me with this?"

Many hands make light work, so lend me yours.

Attention to detail is why people get accolades.

Respect yourself and your teammates, too. Everyone has value when they're shown the respect they deserve.

Your salon's culture in action.

You need a really clear understanding of why these values are so worthwhile to your salon and why they're non-negotiable. Then you can use them routinely to resolve issues in your salon, to remind your team what's expected of them. When you find someone not following your culture, trot out one of these guidelines. Example: if someone's faffing about on their phone at the end of the day and not helping in the clean-up process, instead of saying *Can you help us?* refer instead to a guiding principle: *Many hands make light work, so if you could put down your phone and help us, I'd really appreciate it*. Rather than having a shot at them, you're reinforcing an expectation that they're already aware of. It's completely reasonable, non-negotiable and easy to implement.

16

Tackling tough topics like bad breath and sloppy appearance.

I once sent a girlfriend to a salon as a mystery shopper and she was very happy with her cut and colour. What she didn't like was smelling cigarettes on the hairdresser's hands when she was putting the foils in around her face. When I gave feedback to the team member I just mentioned the cigarette smell as one of many things, good and bad, on my list. I also suggested that if she was going to smoke, she'd be best to wash her hands with hot soapy water and follow-up with a fragranced hand cream. Perhaps she might also ask another team member to smell her hands to check when she came back into the salon.

> *"Don't apologise for having to do your job."*

Seems simple, doesn't it? Sure, it's easier to critique someone when you have an opportunity to give them feedback on several things at once, some positive some negative. But it doesn't always work out that way. Sometimes you need to tackle an issue as a one-off.

Most people would run a mile before they could bring up a tough topic like, *Your breath stinks*. If you have no relationship with the person, I see how it's difficult. But I hope it comes through loud and clear in this book that you must have an honest relationship with your team members. If you build trust and a strong rapport, no topic (even the tough ones) should be off limits.

Let's take the example of bad breath. First, get yourself in the right frame of mind. Remember there's probably not a person on the planet who hasn't eaten something that produces stinky breath. Garlic is the number one culprit. And you wouldn't deny anyone a fabulous Italian meal flavoured with lovely garlic, would you? A dental nurse once asked me if we had any restrictions on the foods we could eat the nights before we worked. I thought she was nuts! No boss of mine was going to tell me what I can and can't eat. I see bad breath as an issue you can resolve rather than prevent.

Don't make a big fuss about how difficult it is for you to say this. Take a relaxed but direct approach and don't stare at the person's face waiting for a reaction. You might try something like this:

Maybe there was some garlic in your dinner last night so I think you'll need to keep popping mints today. There's some heavy-duty mouthwash out the back under the kitchen sink – you can use that, too.

Don't apologise for having to do your job. It's a bit like removing a band-aid; just get on with it. One pull and it's gone.

If you get some kick-back, just point out: *We're not precious here and if we need to mention garlic breath, we just do it because it's in the best interest of our clients. You're more than welcome to let me know if I should be having a mint, too.*

I don't like confrontation. I don't think many people do. Although I did have a bachelor uncle (note I mentioned bachelor; confronting people isn't the best way to build relationships) who I'm sure enjoyed the whole experience. He used to stomp into our house when I was a kid and make wild accusations like his head was on fire. Dad would pop him back into his delusional box and send him packing. Mum didn't care for his impromptu visits. She gave him zero time but she never once canned him to us or Dad – she completely ignored him.

Confrontational is a harsh word. To confront someone conjures up ideas of aggressive, attacking behaviour like my bad uncle storming into our house. I wish there was a more positive word around unravelling confusion and getting to a point of clarity because that's what you're really doing: bringing clarity to a situation in your salon.

When most of us thought about owning our own salon, our imagination kicked in and wandered off to images of a salon where exceptional service was delivered to awesome clients by a bunch of happy team members. We didn't really give any thought to the shitty stuff we'd have to tackle from time to time, the crappy bits that only the business owner, the leader of the tribe, can address. Nobody teaches you this and nobody tells you about it. But, I'll tell you this – like most things in life, the more you do it, the better you get at it.

> *Sometimes you need to tackle an issue as a one-off.*

Another thing salon owners struggle with is the way our team members present themselves. Personal presentation is critical in our industry. The difference between a beautiful makeup application and a rough-and-ready job is incredible. We need to understand that our clients look to us for style. If you don't have any, how the hell can you hope to gain the respect of your clients?

Some salons have uniforms because they struggle to help team members make good decisions for themselves around their clothing choices. Uniforms seem to be far more acceptable in the beauty sector and many people like a uniform because they don't have to think about what to wear to work. Be warned, though: you can certainly score a four out of ten, even in a uniform. Your hair and your makeup still need to be above an eight, or even better, a nine.

An action plan for tackling sloppy appearance.

Often when team members look good we don't say a word. Yet, whenever they let their standards drop, we feel the need to point it out. With this thinking you're highlighting the poorer behaviour. You'd be better doing it the other way around and making a fuss when a team member looks great:

That's a great pair of pants you're wearing.

That colour looks so good on you.

I love that lipstick shade on you. What's it called?

Go a step further and ask your team members to give themselves a score out of 10 for presentation each day. Let's assume as the leader you never ever drop below a nine. You might lose a point for chipped nail polish or shoes that could do with a lick of polish. A point (or two!) for having a bad hair day only because it's due. The list goes on. When you look your absolute best, you get 10.

At any point you could stop and say to your team "Random number check, guys!" Give each a post-it note with another team member's name on it and ask them to score each other. Share the results but don't ask the team to explain their scores to each other. Let them reflect on their own score – chances are they know why they got the score they did; they were just hoping to get away with it! A random, once-a-week check is a great way to keep on top of it. You could have a surprise gift for anyone who scores a 10 – this could be as simple as letting them choose a product off the shelf or leave an hour early. They love that one and it really costs you ZIP.

The Nitty Gritty.

Without a solid salon culture, you will never have the freedom you crave.

Get clear about who does what and when.

Set your salon's culture out in a succinct list of values. Refer to them often.

Make sure everyone on your team understand your expectations.

Build trust and rapport – then no topic is off limits.

Get yourself in the right frame of mind.

Confrontation is about bringing clarity to a situation in your salon.

Don't apologise for doing your job.

The more you do it, the better you get.

Introduce a random check for team members' appearance.

chapter 17

17

Why they're leaving you and what should you do ... pay more, talk more or let them go?

17

Team members are human. They leave a salon for the same reason they leave any relationship. They believe things have changed, it's no longer the place it used to be. This might or might not be true, but in their eyes it's absolutely true. They feel the give and take is uneven, things are unbalanced, lopsided or not fair. They feel they're giving more than they get. They simply can't tolerate it any longer. They feel there's no future for them here, that things are out of whack. They feel they have no option other than to leave.

When a team member decides to leave your salon, go back to the reasons why they came to work for you in the first place.

They believe things have changed and those reasons are no longer valid. The training may have changed, your brand may have changed, or maybe you've changed your approach.

With any relationship – professional or personal – we tend to look at things through a filter because we're optimistic by nature. Hair and beauty professionals are taught to look for opportunity in whatever situation they're working. That view of the world draws us to this career in the first place. We see things we can improve and that we can be a part of the process that makes things look better than when we arrived. We want to help someone bring out their best and it's no different when we're looking for a place to work.

Your brand is what draws new team members to your business. If your brand resonates with them, they will look more closely. It might be as simple as a recycling policy, your presence in the community or that you do charitable work. The type of clientele you have also reflects your brand. Your price point reflects your brand. For whatever reason, they see themselves as a part of your brand, they feel they'd fit in, and they feel they can help you develop your brand. People want to feel they can contribute to the bigger picture – they want to be part of a movement, a community, a family or a tribe.

The sense of a similar mindset is super important. Most people want their talents to be noticed. They want to be in a place where they aren't going to be ridiculously over-skilled or severely under-skilled. They need to see themselves fitting in.

When someone starts working with you, they're on their best behaviour and nothing seems to be too much trouble. If only we could spray them in hair lacquer in those first few days so that it sets and they never change. I wish.

Think of it like any romantic relationship – in the beginning, nothing is too much trouble and you always wear your best knickers, just in case. Both of you happily go out of your way to listen to the other. You answer the phone before it rings twice and you're very attentive. If there's a chance you can help the other person in any way, you will. Minty breath. Manners. The works.

For the most part, you're happy to spend time doing not much at all; just being in each other's company is enough. You're interested in what the other person has to say and open to seeing their point of view. It doesn't mean you agree, but you'll always listen with an open mind.

You and I both know that in the beginning of a romantic relationship, we've all been known to do things we don't really care to do. For example, I went to a football match when I first started dating Simon and I haven't been to one since (I always seem to have something more important to do, like writing this book).

So here's the kicker: if you could just adopt that way of thinking – that new relationship approach – with every team member in your salon, you'll be well on the path to being an employer of choice. And, who wants to leave an employer of choice?

Keeping the love alive in your salon.

Keep the two-way "fresh love" feeling alive in your salon by creating an environment where everyone feels heard and valued. Reinforce the feeling over and over in weekly one-on-one meetings and full team meetings. Week-in, week-out, forever.

Don't tell me you've stopped having meetings because you have nothing to talk about. As leader of the tribe, it's your job to find things to talk about and content to share. It could be as simple as a motivational quote you read somewhere or a question used as a starting point. You need a theme for the week and a plan.

Your question might be:

If you had a spare two hours in the salon, what would you do to make it a better place?

What are you working on and where are you winning?

If this was your salon, what's the first thing you'd change?

> **"As the leader of your salon you need to be the person who promotes good, fresh thinking."**

If you go to **www.yoursalonteam.com.au/resources**, you can download more questions you can use to spark meaningful conversations with your team members

As the leader of your salon you need to be the person who not only solves the challenges day-in day-out but also promotes good, fresh thinking. Your thinking determines your outcome. If you think you can, you can and if you think you can't, you can't. Either way you are correct.

The quality of your thoughts determines the quality of your outcomes.

The trouble is that most of your thoughts are ones you already had; they come from what happened in the past. In simple terms, they are yesterday's thoughts.

We all know that if we feed our bodies with exceptionally fresh food – food that hasn't been tampered with, has the least amount of packaging and minimal processing – this gives us our best results. We feel energised and more alive. Bouncy, even.

We need to feed our brains the same way. If all our thoughts are the same as the day before or the month before or the year before, we'll become stale and set in our ways. Sometimes, you listen to someone or you read someone else's point of view and it absolutely resonates with you. Not because it reflects your own thinking, but because it's different thinking. That's the exciting part and the brain food, right there! And that's exactly why I'm writing this book: new brain food for you.

When you work with anyone, there's a relationship. What you both need to do is take ownership of that relationship. It's a two-way street. You need to communicate well, feel that you can trust each other and be honest with what you're feeling so the other person understands your point of view. If you don't make time to communicate, cracks will start to appear and one day out of the blue, someone says, *We need to talk.* As a business owner, your stomach sinks because you know what's coming – a resignation.

If you communicate openly and every week, if you spend 20 minutes together talking about all kinds of things including the mindset of your team members, you won't need to worry about a *We need to talk* conversation. You'll have an engaged, valued and loyal team who want to stay in the relationship. Most people struggle with consistent meetings and it's just so important that you do.

Paying your team: too much, too little or just right?

Have you ever seen an overfed cat? They're not about to chase their lunch. Why would they? They can hang around that self-feeder any old time they're feeling hungry and get as much kitty food as they want. Some of the pickier ones refuse to eat any food other than a particular brand. So the owner goes back to the supermarket for a refund, apologising at the service counter for their finicky pet. Crazy! I used to cut a pilot's hair whose wife once told me she'd just started shopping at Aldi. She was laughing because her husband was happily drinking the Aldi red wine but one of her two cats refused to eat the Aldi cat food. She told me that it wasn't the moggy cat, it was the British blue. Hilarious that a cat would know its pedigree.

What do cats and your staff have in common?

Like cats, salon staff shouldn't be overindulged. There should be some reward for catching and killing your own. Otherwise, why would they bother?

My brother told me once that he heard a speaker at a seminar say that if you treat your team well, they will hang around for more of the same, just like cats do. They look at any employment situation with a "what's in it for me" approach. They're not like dogs – so loyal they'll stay by your side no matter how you treat them. It's an interesting analogy, though I believe, like in most things, the best way to keep your team loyal is finding a balance in what you pay them.

A fine balance.

To me, a great pay is a balance between a good base rate or retainer and a performance-based pay. Everyone on your team needs to feel financially secure. That usually includes having a steady reliable income so they meet their financial commitments and knowing they'll be looked after if they become sick.

In Australia we still value, more than most countries in the world, owning our own home. When your team member is ready, they need to be able to prove a consistent income so they can secure a bank loan or mortgage. They need (and deserve) a steady rate of pay. I often come across people who rent a chair from the salon owner and battle to qualify for any sort of finance because the bank considers them a risk as a contractor.

Most of us would struggle after three months of being off work due to illness. The solution is income protection. Sadly, people don't understand much about income protection insurance, even though we all get that we need to insure our car. We're taught how difficult it would be to manage without a car but rarely are we educated about the difficulty of having no income. That's mad – no income means no car, no house, no food and it's a scary thought.

I've had income protection for years and years. My accountant not only suggested I should, but bothered to explain how dangerous it was not to have it. In my experience, many contractors who work in salons don't even manage to take four weeks a year for holidays because they can't afford it. The security a wage brings to each of your team members is very valid.

Then, there needs to be an opportunity for your exceptional team members to understand their true value to your business. You know who I mean – the ones who go over and above when it comes to customer service and delivering an outstanding experience every time. Your clients might love your shop fit-out but don't kid yourself – they come to your salon for two things. They want a great experience and they want an expert. If you deliver both you'll develop a loyal clientele for your business.

Your challenge as salon owner is to find a fine balance, so you don't develop lazy, fat cat team members. By making the base pay too high, your team members could be lulled into a false sense of entitlement and become lazy. If you introduce any sort of financial bonus for them, they have an incentive to perform and improve.

A great pay – one that is not too much, not too little and just right – combines a good base pay and a performance-boosting bonus system. You definitely need both components to achieve the best outcomes for your business.

17

Yikes! Everyone's leaving.

One of my sisters had her heart broken when her husband left her for another woman when their two boys were babies, the youngest just 18 months old. He left because he was having an affair with someone he met through the football club. Her world was turned upside down. She was devastated and really struggled to move on. Soon after, our mum's heart was also broken when our dad passed away. I hadn't thought about the similarity of the emotions they were both going through. Not until Mum pointed it out one day when my sister was trying to explain how horrible and alone she felt.

"I feel exactly the same way," Mum said. "But we have to move on, get used to it."

My sister replied, "Dad died. My husband cheated on me. It's so different."

"No, it's not. They've both gone and neither of them will be back."

I thought long and hard about that. It was pretty brave of Mum to say it so matter-of-factly at the time. If I'd said it, my sister would have taken a bite out of my face like it was a shiny red apple. I'm often saying things that get me into trouble.

It was a good lesson for me. If we could take that approach whenever a staff member leaves our salon – for whatever reason – and accept that they've gone and they won't be back, we'd be much more able to move on and get on with business.

As salon owner, you need to be always looking ahead, having a plan for the next person you need on your team. The more time you waste thinking about how bad the timing is for that team member to leave – how much you did for them, how ungrateful they were, what rubbish you had to put up with – the more you'll be stuck. Right there, where you are: down a pair of hands. It's the sort of negative thinking that slows you down and stops you, as Mum said, getting on with it.

> *Accept that they've gone and they won't be back.*

The emotion of the situation paralyses you from moving forward. I don't want that for you. We all get there in the end but we need to learn faster and not take situations so personally. When someone doesn't want to work with you anymore, your next thought needs to be about your plan of moving forward without them. So, stop wallowing in what was or what might have been. Pull on your big girl undies or your tough guy jocks and get on with your next move. It may be your best yet.

Honestly, are you too scared to let them go?

This, I know for sure: if you're not completely honest with yourself, it will absolutely bite you in the arse. You might get away with it for a while, perhaps even years, but I guarantee, at some stage, it will either wear you down or bring you down.

In business, that means your salon either fails to thrive or fails. Full stop. You need to understand that leading your salon tribe is firmly anchored to honesty.

There are two ways to be dishonest. One is telling a lie. The other is holding back information. Either way, whatever the deception, it will bite you.

Over the years, I've worked with salon owners who, once they got comfortable and told me what was really going on, were painting themselves into remarkably tight corners. You paint yourself into a corner when one white lie leads to another. Then another. At first, you might not even think it's a lie because the person you're lying to is you. Before you know it, you've let something slide, which leads you to another decision you're not happy about until you wake up one morning and don't even want to go into your own business because you can't stand some of the people on your team.

Perhaps they're ungrateful or difficult communicators or have any one of a hundred other qualities you dislike in a person. Then someone from the outside looks in and says: *Why do you put up with this person? Why do you take that kind of bullying from this obnoxious individual?*

From my experience, it's usually because they make you money and you're scared to unravel this big ball of knots you created. You can't see where it starts or where it ends.

So you continue on with this toxic relationship, telling yourself that one day you can sell-up and leave it all behind you. This might happen. It might not. Meanwhile, you're living and working inside a ticking time bomb. I'm squirming just thinking about it!

Often when I start with a new salon and begin my process of introducing changes to the way a team thinks, I ask questions about why one or two team members aren't included in the learning. I see unhealthy deals between a particular staff member and the business owner. Sure, the salon owner always has their reason to justify this operator who floats around the business like they have some golden ticket that exempts them from the rules.

You need to understand that your clients (and the general public) don't know this. From the outside, this person represents your brand. These toxic team members never pull their weight and people notice. They don't recommend retail homecare for their clients or offer basin services simply because they're set in their ways. Invariably, most of their sentences begin with, "I know …"

Why do you let them sponge off you?

What scares you so much about the prospect of them leaving? Of course, they'll take some of their clientele with them and you'll miss out on that regular income. But what you won't miss out on is that horrible feeling of having your wheels clamped by this team member.

The best thing you can do is to let them know that by a particular time or date, their services will no longer be required. This person is doing your business more harm than you can imagine. The example they set for your team and the vibe they give off to your customers is doing you far more damage than you know.

If you're keeping someone on who you know doesn't represent your brand and you're paying them to stay because you're scared if they leave, you've locked yourself into a relationship built on money and money alone. If you know this person is incapable of change – and I bet you already know – you don't even have to think about it. You know the answer. Instead, think about creating a strategy around when it suits you to give this person their notice to leave. It might take you six months to get your head around it, but trust me, it will end up in tears if you don't.

If the only reason you're in business is money, then you won't be able to sustain it. Yet, the only reason you're tolerating this person is money. Right there, you have an internal conflict. You're not being honest with the person who matters most – you.

The Nitty Gritty.

People leave because thing have changed.

As in any relationship, your team members want to feel valued and heard.

Keep the love alive in weekly meetings. Never stop having weekly meetings. Not ever.

Ask questions to spark meaningful conversations.

Pay too much, and your people may become lazy.

Find the balance of base pay and performance bonuses.

When a team member leaves, don't take it personally.

Face up to it: they've gone and they won't be back.

Get on with finding your next team member.

Be honest with yourself about your team.

The lies you tell yourself will bring you down.

chapter 18

18

Get clear on who your clients belong to.

Imagine an army of termites chomping away at the foundations of your salon business without you knowing they're there. That's the sort of destruction that happens when you allow your team members to think about your clients as theirs. The "termites" arrive without warning and, before you know it, you're hurled into full damage control to fix a problem that should never have occurred in the first place.

In most salons, the whole issue of who the clients belong to is a mess. For some reason, we let our staff refer to our salon clients as "mine" – crazy!

How did our industry end up so unprofessional? When did it all begin? Who says it's OK to do this? When it comes to taking clients from previous employers we are world-class. I have a clean slate here – I can honestly say I didn't do it. I was told at the very start of my career that it's not what you do.

So, where does this practice even come from?

Maybe it comes from us encouraging team members to build relationships with their clients so that they can develop a trust with stylist or beauty therapist. Changing somebody's physical appearance relies heavily on trust. Building a rapport with someone is very important to both the client and you as the operator. Once you establish the trust you can really do you best work and give your client the outcomes they want in solving their hair and beauty challenges. I guess it's an easy progression for a team member to flow on from that relationship to using the word "mine" about your clients.

As salon owners, we also encourage new team members to bring clients with them. Some even advertise for people who have their own client base. Of course, clients are free to come and go as they please so it's up to us, as professionals, to do two things. First: stop making clients feel bad if they get a cut from your salon and a colour elsewhere in another salon. Second: educate your clients that there is more than one person within your salon who can look after them. Make them feel comfortable and empowered about their ability to choose.

It's never *mine*, it's always *ours*. The same as it's never *I*, it's always *we*.

At some stage, when you were just starting out in this industry, you didn't have a clientele at all. The only people you got to look after were those who walked in off the street or the random person who called up last minute. Remember how hard you worked at getting those clients to rebook with you so that you could start to say those magic words, "my client"?

While you were still learning the ropes, you were given the opportunity to assist someone else more experienced than you. When you became competent, someone handed you over some of their clients (usually the ones they didn't particularly like doing – all guilty of that one). As luck would have it, some of those clients preferred your work and that's how, in your mind, you came to believe that they were *your* clients. They actually asked for you, so that made you think they were *yours*.

The trouble with that thinking is you haven't considered that the owner of the business marketed to those clients. They paid for a website, a brochure, flyers and business cards. They fitted out a shop. They paid the salon's GST and taxes, the salon's rent and all of the expenses that come with owning a business.

And, they had all the joys and stresses of owning a business thrown in for free! Yes, darling, there are your steak knives right there. You can have this (a salon business) and you can have the bonus STRESS and sleepless nights, too.

I'll give you an example. You can also think you're having a day off and at the last minute, because someone on the team calls in sick, your day Plan A is now Plan B. Yes, darling, there are your steak knives again, right there. That's the bonus that you hadn't counted on. Laughing or crying, it's true and you know it is.

While all this is happening your team members who've been given these clients to look after, these opportunities to advance their skills, have decided that the clients actually belong to them! Then, for some reason or another, something happens and this employee decides not to work in your business anymore. They leave and think that it's okay to take what they believe to be their clients with them. Yep, they take them to either another salon or (worse still) to their own home. They seem to have forgotten that the clients belong to the salon. Your salon!

How do you prevent this happening? You must be completely open and upfront about who the clients belong to and promote a culture where you *ALL* look after the salon's clients as a team. This is the only way you can protect yourself from watching your clients follow a team member when they leave your business.

> *Educate your clients* **that there is** *more than one person* **within your** *salon* **who can look after them.**

While you continue to use the "one client only gets to know and use the services of one team member" model, you're putting your business at risk when that team member leaves – and they will leave. Everyone leaves eventually. It's just a matter of when. You need to be keep one step ahead by sharing the clients across your team.

When clients come into your salon, make sure they're "touched" by more than one person; two or three is ideal. I'll give you an example. In hairdressing, someone cuts and another person colours and someone else does the basin work including one of those beautiful head massages. The client is still the sole responsibility of the person who is the cutter and this stylist works closely with the other team members – together they engage the client, but one person oversees the whole project. It's time-efficient and shows your clients the depth of expertise across your team. When you lose one of your team, your client still has a relationship with the other team members, significantly increasing your chances of retaining the client.

Beware the one-man survey.

Some of you'll be thinking:

But my clients don't like this. They like having only have one operator looking after them. They've been to salons where more than one operator works on them, and they don't like it.

This thinking is a classic example of the one-man survey, where one person tells you something and you decide to believe it's true. If you think a little deeper you'll question whether the client's reaction was more about the *way* their visit was handled rather than the *fact* that the services was shared across multiple team members. If the sharing isn't handled well, of course a bad client experience will result. Often, the only time you share your clients with your team members is when you're desperate. You throw someone in to do something when they're not properly trained. No wonder your clients don't appreciate it! You have to get it right. For example, what would be wrong with two seniors putting foils in at the same time? Nothing, except the client would get out on time or even ahead of schedule. Instead of having people standing around and chatting to you while you're working, get them to pick up a tail comb and help you place your foils. Fifteen minutes is very helpful and goes a long way on a busy day. And it helps you bring in that culture of one, in all in.

My, my, my, mine.

Every time you hear someone refer to a client as *mine* or *my*, I want you to correct them. People don't own people (not in this country, anyway). People are free to come and go as they please, clients are no different. We all need to respect that they can choose to have their hair and beauty services done wherever they like. It's none of our business, unless they choose your salon. If they choose your salon, how they're treated is every bit your team's business. I really don't like the way some team members don't take any notice of you because "you're not their next client."

I remember going to visit a new beauty salon coaching client. We'd spoken on the phone a couple of times but I'd not met anyone on her team, nor had I ever been into her salon so no one knew who I was. I went in, sat down and waited – I always like to see how long it takes for someone to notice me. The staff were all busy seeing clients in and out and had no idea I was watching like a hawk. When the owner of the beauty salon came out and introduced me they were very apologetic saying that they didn't know I was the new coach. They just thought I was a client. Which is actually worse because if they thought I was a client, why on earth did they ignore me?

The answer was, "We thought you were for Emma". What? That's just crazy. "You're telling me you're only spoiling and looking after those who are directly in your column?" I said. "You don't look after everyone who comes in? There is your problem – single vision. Your only-looking-out-for-me BS is killing the team one in, all in rule."

Every one of you must've done your training somewhere with someone at some stage. That's how you built your first clientele. That person owned a business just like you. What should happen is, when you leave, you should move just a little too far away for your clients to follow and leave your clients in the salon where they belong. True?

At every opportunity make sure your team remembers who the clients belong to. To reinforce the thinking, write a list of all the people who came to your salon because of each particular team member and their previous relationship in a previous business. It may be that the clients genuinely do belong to that person because she had a salon of her own and closed the doors for some reason. That's different. If he or she sold the business, then the clients should be staying with the original salon as part of the sale.

Can you stop people from stealing clients? NO, you can't. Can you educate them to understand your point of view as a business owner? Absolutely. Yes, you can and you should. If we all did this as an industry starting today, being open and talking about this at the beginning of anyone's employment and making it crystal clear, things will slowly

> **Promote a culture where you ALL look after the salon's clients as a team.**

There's an old saying: *If they do it for you, then they will also do it to you.* Remember that when they offer to bring their client's with them.

The more open you are, the more honest you are, and the more you can say: *I never did that to my boss. I know it's the wrong thing to do and I don't want you to do that either.*

Then you have a leg to stand on. Everything I know about teams is based on being a great example to those on your team. That's what great leadership is. It's very different to management.

I don't think you can manage people. I think you can manage the systems within your business, but not the people. You have to be their leader. Think of it this way: if someone says, "I want to be the manager of this salon" swap that word for the "leader" and see if they still want the gig. Does anyone ever come to you and say, "I want to be the leader. I want everyone to look at me as the way things need to done"? (I'll tell you more about that in the next chapter.)

Sometimes they're really saying: "I want to be the person to tell people what to do" rather than the person who is a living example of how to go about what to do. Showing people what to do by example is very, very different to telling.

The Nitty Gritty.

Your salon clients belong to your salon.

Stop allowing your team to think of clients as "theirs."

Promote a culture where you ALL look after the salon's clients as a team.

Stop asking new team members to bring clients with them.

Lead by example to show it's not on.

chapter 19

19

Is there a potential salon manager or partner in your midst?

More often than not, senior members in our teams want to be the manager. Mostly they have no idea what the word manager even means, and they don't care to step-up. They just want the badge. They want to be able to go home to their grandma and say "Guess what, Gran, I'm the salon manager!"

In my opinion, part of the reason they covet the role is because our salons don't offer many steps for people to climb. Every time they read a Cleo magazine or do quizzes about how they're progressing at work, they feel driven to be part of the "important people crowd" and in their eyes, that's being the salon manager.

Sometimes when I'm working closely with a salon owner they say to me, "I've got this girl and she's come to me and said she wants to be the manager. Can I groom her to be the manager?" My answer is, "Yes, you can do anything if you put your mind to it."

At the same time, I find it fascinating that they're reacting to what the team member wants, rather than what their business needs. It's the wrong way around.

I say to them:

Get two sheets of paper, one for you and one for this girl. Sit there together for five minutes and fill in the rest of this sentence. The manager role is …

Then we get to see if they're speaking the same language when it comes to the role. Most salon owners will say to me after I fish around a little bit, that they want someone to be responsible for the salon when they're not there. They want someone who will dob the team in when they slacken off. They want someone to take responsibility if things go pear-shaped and they want the true story relayed back to them. In short, they want them to be their replacement when they're not there.

That's not always the way the team member sees the role. Most want to get their "inner bossy" out and boss a couple of people around. They have no idea how bad that thinking really is.

It doesn't sit well with me that the team member who wants to be salon manager is often the same team member who sees the most clients and brings in the most money for the business each week. They have the biggest workload and they want to increase it. Being salon manager means you can't run a full book. Depending how capable they are, the responsibilities of salon manager would need for them to reduce their client time by five hours or maybe 10 hours each week. For big teams, it might require 20 hours a week.

The salon manager pay is not much more than a team member's, so why would someone who already has the biggest workload want to take on extra responsibility for all that's going on around them? Where you'll get paid more in most salons is by having a full book of clients week in, week out. What are they really asking when they want to be the Manager? I say: they just want to wear a badge.

The other challenge we have is that, unlike other industries, most people who manage our salons don't come in from the outside. They have to make a shift from being a regular team member one day, to being the manager the next. Most people work their way up the ranks and they get asked to do this job because they're good, honest and loyal people who you can trust. Their playmates, the team members they've been working alongside for many years may not feel as positive about the change. They almost always seem to have their noses out of joint because they're weren't themselves chosen to wear the badge. I know of cases where giving the management role to one of your key people, meant losing another team member equally as great because they felt undervalued.

So, be careful giving people the honour (and responsibility) of the salon manager badge. I'd consider inviting every senior on your team to write a 300-words-or-less essay about why they'd like to be manager. That way, all your seniors have at least been invited. I'd also make available a list of tasks that they'd be expected to undertake as salon manager. Most of them will be frightened away by the level of responsibility and start to wonder if that badge is worth all that effort. Except, of course, for the one who really wants the job for all the right reasons. And, that's the one you need to focus on.

Is a partnership right for you?

One of the biggest challenges we face in our industry is that our great people, our exceptional team members, often leave us. The best we can hope for is that they don't take our clients with them and open up a salon across the road.

It happened to me and I was gutted. It took me months to get over it. My business survived but it took some time. I don't know how many times I tried to climb back up from the low it dropped me in.

My situation was a little different because this person was leaving to go into business with her mother and her sister. For $6,000 they bought a business that was closed down due to the previous owner's financial mess. The move wasn't planned. It was sprung upon me. And I certainly had no prior intentions of opening a second salon with that particular team member in mind. In fact, I hadn't really thought about a second store, mainly because most of my team were young and not looking to be business owners. My oldest team member was 26 years old.

Before I became a salon owner, I worked for one man for 16 years. I remember telling him that I wanted to have my own salon and I'd be happy to have one in some sort of arrangement with him. He was a traditional Italian man, very set in his ways, and had been burnt before in a previous partnership. I couldn't convince him that a partnership between us would be different.

So when I was ready, I left. His business suffered because although my salon was some 50km away there were some people who just decided not to go back to the business. They felt that without me, it was never going to be the same. We lost them even though I didn't take them – some people see it as a chance to try another place.

It's easy to open up your own salon particularly in hairdressing because the fit-out and set-up costs are quite affordable. If we're talking high-end beauty, it's not so easy – you need to invest hundreds of thousands of dollars in equipment before you can even open your doors. I wish it were the same in the hair industry.

It takes years to get a business to where it's consistent and the income is steady. Not reproducing that business model in another location is a real shame. You've done so much of the work already and you can easily replicate it in another location. You have all your product providers. You've chosen your software, your furniture and your artwork. You've developed your marketing plan, your training calendar and your strong culture.

Yet, what prevents most people going into a partnership with an employee is the fear of what might go wrong. It stops you before you even begin. It really shouldn't be that hard. You need to be honest with each other, set up an exit strategy that covers either of you getting out of the partnership because of a number of clearly documented reasons.

I can't think of an industry other than hairdressing where there are so many one-off businesses. Cafés, restaurants and florists are probably next on the list and it's interesting that they're also businesses where owners very often have a creative mindset. Travel agencies, drycleaners, bookstores and even opp shops seem to have all slowly changed from single operating stores to bigger chain stores repeated in multiple sites over multiple suburbs. There are fewer and fewer one-off clothing boutiques as the big guys seem to be conquering the market with multiple stores and, of course, with super-efficient online shopping.

> **You need to be *honest with each other*, set up an *exit strategy* that covers either of you getting out of the partnership.**

Why would you want two businesses (or babies) like that?

Sometimes when I'm working on setting up a business plan for a salon owner, I'm surprised to find they have a big picture goal to have a second salon. More often than not, the income stream in their existing salon is inconsistent or unreliable. Why would you want two businesses like that? I explain that wanting a second salon is absolute madness at this stage.

Imagine if you had a baby. Now imagine your baby's not sleeping through the night. You have to keep getting up during the night and putting the dummy in to get baby back to sleep. Would you like to add to your already sleepless night? Wouldn't you want to wait until this baby is at least sleeping more nights than not before you go and get yourself another one? I thought so. Let's get this baby popping its own dummy back in its own mouth and into some sort of routine. Then you'll know when it will sleep, when it needs feeding and when it will be awake. Then, and only then, should you be looking at baby number two. That seems to sink in and they don't ask me again. Instead we shift the "salon number two" idea to the backburner and get on with the task of taking salon number one from good to great.

By the way, as a mother of twins, I know only too well the two babies scenario.

The Nitty Gritty.

Understand why you want a salon manager.

Understand why your team member wants the role.

Make sure it's about more than wearing the badge.

Think about partnering to replicate your salon.

Wait until your salon is consistent and reliable.

Set up an exit strategy with your partner.

chapter 20

20

Stop beating yourself up. You *can* learn to lead your tribe.

Leadership is not in our DNA. Less than 5% of the population are natural born leaders. It makes sense – imagine if it was the reverse with 95% of the world born leaders and only 5% of them followers. That has disaster written all over it!

The great thing is that I know leadership is something you can learn. It takes time, lots of practice and plenty of mistakes (or learning lessons, as I call them). So stop beating yourself up about what you weren't born with and start learning what you need to know to be a kick-arse salon owner.

Many years ago when I started working with my first coach, he did a personality profile on me. I was a little nervous about what he might find. He was more surprised than I was when the results came back. He thought the profile would show I had more leadership qualities. Instead I had what he called a classic hairdresser or beauty therapist personality.

There are many psychometric/behavioural tests. They come in all shapes and sizes. The one I use and have found great results with is the DISC.

There are four main DISC personality categories and everyone has a little bit of each.

D stands for a dominant personality

I is for a person of influence

S represents a supportive person

C means a compliant person

There are two results when you complete this profile – one is in your natural state at home amongst those you're most comfortable with; the other represents you in the workplace. Although they can be completely different, almost every profile I've ever done has shown that for the most part people are the same at work as at home. There is actually very little acting. We surround ourselves with certain people at work and at home because we genuinely like it that way.

What came through for me in my very first profile was my incredibly high score in I/influence. A person with a high I/influence score cares what other people think about them.

Your Salon Team

We're people pleasers and we run from person to person trying to keep the peace. We're only really happy when everyone else is happy. You and I both know the trouble with that thinking in a salon – it's impossible to please everyone and there's no real leader. A room full of followers with no leader has "tits up" written all over it.

When I did this test my mentor thought I'd have been much higher in D/dominant, meaning he thought I was a driven person. He felt that I could decide what I wanted and set about getting it done. Part of that's true but I kept falling over by constantly trying to please my team. When I felt they weren't happy, I'd go back and do my best to change things. I'd re-think it and make yet another decision and another plan. This caused a real conflict in my head, which I found exhausting.

When I put my hand up for some help, I knew what I wanted to know, but how to go about getting it was another story. Over the years, I've worked really hard on changing my personality profile. Now, at work I have learnt to be more driven and more precise, more focused and more systemised, because I see the value it brings to my team and to my business.

Most people I work with are excitable and spasmodic, with high energy levels. It's easy to get lured off the track when you're surrounded by an energised team. As leader, I need to be the person sticking to the plan and not letting them deviate.

> *"Leadership is something you can learn. It takes time, lots of practice and plenty of mistakes."*

At home in my natural habitat and relaxed state I'm exactly that original profile. I'm a very high I/influence personality, the same person I've always been. I simply learnt to adjust. And you can learn, too. Most people I've DISC profiled come up with very little D/dominant or C/compliant. They usually score really high in I/influence or S/supportive.

It's difficult for these personality types to lead a team – they're exactly like me. Making people happy is their first priority. Being supportive to their clients and their colleagues means they please everyone else first and then they burn out.

But, someone has to lead the team and it might as well be you! You have a vision for what you want and you can do this. You have to be less sensitive around making sure that everyone else is happy. Once you get that you can't please everyone, you can really start making the smart decisions that will lead your team and your business to a new level of success.

More about DISC.

The way I explain DISC profiles is by asking salon owners to imagine they're planning a work party. Here's what the different DISC personality categories are likely to bring to the party planning table.

D – dominant

The D personality makes their own decision on where the party should be, deciding quickly and telling the group where and when the party is going to be. They don't give much thought about whether it's where the team would like to go. The D personality is very busy and can't see the point in wasting time on small detail. "It's $50 ahead and I need to know by tomorrow who is coming and who's not." And don't ask what you get for your $50 – D type hasn't bothered to check. They've already moved on to solving another problem.

D personalities are known for "getting shit done" and often seen in key roles like the CEO of a big company.

I – influence

The I personality tends to get carried away with making the party fancy dress. They go around chatting with everyone, changing the theme every time someone comes up with a better idea. They spend time asking everyone where they think is a good venue and get excited about how much fun it's going to be. They often paint themselves into a corner because they can't please everyone and it ends in tears. They give up and hand over to someone else because they don't want the drama, never understanding that they caused the drama in the first place

I personalities are also found in the airline flight crew staff – they need to build a rapport with people very quickly and so being liked is very important to them.

S – supportive

The S personality is concerned that we need some vegetarian or vegan options and that the starting time mightn't give those with children enough time to get ready. "Do you think we should ask if some people would like their partners along?" They're very thoughtful and always happiest when supporting other people.

S personalities make great nurses – they have the largest group of friends I know and they seem to keep these friends their whole life.

C – compliant

The C personality thinks that last year's venue was just fine. They think we'd be better to just go there again because we know what we'll get. They like the detail and they're not keen on surprises. Unless it's broken, they'd prefer not to change things, just in case.

C personalities make great accountants – it's why your accountant's office never gets refurbished; it's not broken and technically it still functions with the ugly 30-year-old chairs and outdated magazines.

Over the years I did come across a couple of personalities that were high in either D or C categories. One that comes to mind was a girl I employed for less than 12 months. She really struggled fitting into the team. Her compliance side was one out-of-the-box and quite hilarious to watch.

She could put foils in a head of hair like a machine. She had a method of doing foils and nobody could convince her to do it any other way. She placed and folded those foil packages up so beautifully, it seemed a shame they had to come out 20 minutes later.

She lacked a sense of humour and didn't care how much fun the girls poked at her precise foil work. She didn't care for anyone else's opinion and was not about to change her method. Like I said, not your average garden variety of hairdresser. I might add she didn't stay in the industry; she never really enjoyed the people interaction. I always thought she'd have worked well with an anaesthetist – putting in people's foils when they're asleep would have been perfect for her!

For me as a salon owner, she was a breeze to work with – no highs and lows, just a repetitive little machine. You got the same service every single time.

The Nitty Gritty.

There are few natural born leaders.

You *can* learn what you need to lead.

Discover your personality profile and start working on it.

chapter 21

21

Tits up, in a good way?

It was a Thursday evening and I was at home doing paperwork. I no longer worked on the salon floor, so I could pretty much do what I liked, whenever I liked. Claire my salon manager called and said, "Are you sitting down? You won't believe the offer I've got for you."

She explained that Sarita (one of her regular clients) had planned a five-day Whitsundays yachting holiday to celebrate her fortieth birthday with a small group of girlfriends. One friend had pulled out at the last minute. The return airfare, the yacht, everything was paid for.

"What a shame, I don't know anyone who can possibly drop everything and come along on such short notice?" said Sarita.

"Lisa can!" said Claire. I thought about it (for just a split-second) and realised, "Yes, I can, why not?"

That night I packed my bags. The next day I popped into my salon and checked my team was right to manage while I was away. They waved me off with, "Go, enjoy yourself. You've earned it."

Years earlier, when I worked on my salon floor, I was trapped. When I didn't work, the money stopped. If I wasn't the prime person earning the clients' trust and building relationships, there was no money. So, there were no holidays for me. No freedom. No choices.

It didn't take me long to work out I needed a team. What I wanted to achieve most through having a team was more freedom. Most salon owners think about getting a team to have someone to help them out, someone to be with them all day, someone to "play with" as they're working. I always imagined a team being there, always working, even when I wasn't. I wanted a business that would generate income for me, even when I was on holiday.

The Whitsundays trip showed me I'd reached that milestone. And it taught me something else – that people often just need to be shown another way of thinking.

When I accepted Sarita's offer I explained to her that I have only one rule: I sunbake topless. I'd been doing it since my early twenties – I loathed strap marks. If it was OK with her, I planned to be topless the whole time on the yacht.

She laughed and agreed. I hadn't thought about the yacht skipper being a forty-something male, so I used my best manners and asked his permission and he said, "Of course!"

At first, it was just me lying in the warm Queensland sun with my top off and by day five it was all five of the girls. We cooked topless and we danced topless and all five of us had the time of our lives. We had a fabulous, hilarious, liberating time.

I knew then, more than ever, that I wanted to share what I knew about thinking differently, about how building a great salon team can give salon owners just like me the freedom you crave.

I ask you: if you got a call today to take off on a plane tomorrow for a holiday in the sun, could you drop everything and go? Could you even make time to get to the movies with your girlfriends? To have an evening out perhaps once a month?

Maybe you're struggling to get half an hour at the local park with your kids or your pooch?

I'm not here to teach you how to sunbake topless. But like my dog Muriel, we all need to get off that leash and leave behind our narrow world in favour of fresh thinking.

Like I said at the start of this book: it is as it is. Within these pages, I've shared the business smarts you'll need to get cracking on creating your kick-arse salon team, and your kick-arse life.

It's all within your reach: whatever it is that floats your boat. It's yours for the taking, my darlings.

www.ingramcontent.com/pod-product-compliance
Lightning Source LLC
Chambersburg PA
CBHW050306010526
44107CB00055B/2119